Authentic Assessment
in Action

Authentic Assessment in Action

An Everyday Guide for Bringing Learning to Life through Meaningful Assessment

Katie Alaniz
Kristie Cerling

ROWMAN & LITTLEFIELD
Lanham • Boulder • New York • London

Published by Rowman & Littlefield
An imprint of The Rowman & Littlefield Publishing Group, Inc.
4501 Forbes Boulevard, Suite 200, Lanham, Maryland 20706
www.rowman.com

86-90 Paul Street, London EC2A 4NE, United Kingdom

Copyright © 2023 by Katie Alaniz and Kristie Cerling

All rights reserved. No part of this book may be reproduced in any form or by any electronic or mechanical means, including information storage and retrieval systems, without written permission from the publisher, except by a reviewer who may quote passages in a review.

British Library Cataloguing in Publication Information Available

Library of Congress Cataloging-in-Publication Data

Names: Alaniz, Katie, author. | Cerling, Kristie, 1973- author.
Title: Authentic assessment in action : an everyday guide for bringing learning to life through meaningful assessment / Katie Alaniz and Kristie Cerling.
Description: Lanham, Maryland : Rowman & Littlefield, [2023] | Summary: "Authentic Assessment in Action is designed to empower educators to provide highly impactful, consistently engaging, and unquestionably applicable learning opportunities for students"—Provided by publisher.
Identifiers: LCCN 2022053906 (print) | LCCN 2022053907 (ebook) | ISBN 9781475867626 (Cloth) | ISBN 9781475867633 (Paperback) | ISBN 9781475867640 (epub)
Subjects: LCSH: Competency-based education—United States. | Educational evaluation—United States. | Effective teaching—United States. Classification: LCC LC1032 .A43 2023 (print) | LCC LC1032 (ebook) | DDC 371.27/1—dc23/eng/20230104
LC record available at https://lccn.loc.gov/2022053906
LC ebook record available at https://lccn.loc.gov/2022053907

This book is dedicated to the glory of God.

Contents

Preface	ix
Acknowledgments	xi
Introduction	xiii
Chapter 1: Starting with Why: Why Does Authentic Assessment Matter?	1
Chapter 2: Considering Key Findings: What Does the Research Say?	11
Chapter 3: Beginning with the End in Mind: How Do Curricular Frameworks and Student Learning Outcomes Impact Assessment?	21
Chapter 4: Exploring Assessments, Assessments, and More Assessments: Which Assessment Type Should Be Used When?	33
Chapter 5: Making It All Add Up: How Does the Formula for Authentic Learning Apply?	51
Chapter 6: Embracing the Digital Age: How Do Technology Considerations Impact Assessment Strategies?	63

Chapter 7: Finding Joy in the Journey: How Can Authentic
   Assessment Impact Students' (and Educators') Enjoyment
   of Learning? 75

About the Authors 83

Preface

The inspiration for authoring this guidebook developed as a result of numerous shared experiences. We, Katie Alaniz and Kristie Cerling, first met as colleagues at Houston Christian University, in Houston, Texas. Through our time spent investing in the lives of students, we quickly realized our joint passion for providing learners with meaningful, memorable educational experiences. We believe in the power of beginning with the end in mind (Covey, 1989; Wiggins & McTighe, 2005) and starting with WHY (Sinek, 2011) when designing learning opportunities for students, whether in EC–12 or higher education settings.

Both of us have witnessed greater student engagement, motivation, and success as a result of purposeful learning endeavors—learning endeavors that align with everyday life and directly correlate with students' current and future personal and professional pursuits. We believe that as educators, we owe this to our students; they simply spend too many waking hours in school contexts for their time not to be spent wisely. The following guidebook represents the culmination of proven frameworks for purposeful living and learning (Covey, 1989; Wiggins & McTighe, 2005; Sinek, 2011), incorporating key principles from past guidebooks that address the intentional pursuit of impactful authentic assessment endeavors (Wilson, Alaniz, & Sikora, 2016; Alaniz, 2021).

As learners who have benefitted from the tremendous power of authentic assessment in action (as well as endured a number of less purposeful assessment measures), as educators who have taught in a variety of settings spanning from first grade through doctoral programs, and as individuals who believe that all students deserve meaningful learning experiences, we care deeply about empowering others to embrace authentic assessment endeavors.

We have discovered that as we devote less time and energy on achieving academic "to-do's" and instead reflect more intentionally upon "why we do what we do," educational experiences bring greater fulfillment and joy. Teaching and learning should be meaningful, exciting, and joyful. Educators can easily feel like cruise ship activity directors when they lose sight of the end in mind. Because of this, authentic learning endeavors play an important role in purposeful and joy-filled teaching; we hope and pray this will be true of our readers as well.

In the words of King Solomon, widely renowned as the wisest man who ever lived, "Even so, I have noticed one thing, at least, that is good. It is good for people to . . . enjoy their work under the sun" (Ecclesiastes 5:18, *New Living Translation*). Afterall, life is too short to do anything other than this!

REFERENCES

Alaniz, K. (2021). *Collegial coaching: Mentoring for knowledge and skills that transfer to real-world applications.* Lanham, MD: Rowman & Littlefield Education.

Covey, S. R. (1989). *The 7 habits of highly effective people: Restoring the character ethic.* New York: Free Press.

Holy Bible, New Living Translation. Tyndale House Publishers (original work published in 1996).

Sinek, S. (2011). *Start with why.* Harlow, England: Penguin Books.

Wiggins, G., & McTighe, J. (2005). *Understanding by design* (2nd edition). Upper Saddle River, NJ: Pearson/Merrill Education/ASCD. ISBN: 0-205-57860-8

Wilson, D., Alaniz, K., & Sikora, J. (2016). *Digital media in today's classrooms: The potential for meaningful teaching, learning, and assessment.* Lanham, MD: Rowman & Littlefield Education.

Acknowledgments

KATIE'S ACKNOWLEDGMENTS

I would like to convey my deepest gratitude to my incredible husband, Steven (my hero and greatest cheerleader), and to my wonderful family members and friends for consistently being tremendous sources of encouragement and offering faithful prayers throughout every new endeavor. I would also like to wholeheartedly thank those educators who inspired a passion for teaching within my heart, including Mrs. Desi Kelly, Mrs. Patricia McFarlane, and Dr. Dawn K. Wilson (my professor, dear friend, and mentor who inspired and helped develop many of the ideas presented in this book). I am forever grateful to my very first teachers, my wonderful dad and mom.

KRISTIE'S ACKNOWLEDGMENTS

Jon Cerling has always encouraged me to pursue my dreams and goals. When I doubt, he says to go for it—for that, I am grateful. I am thankful for dear friends who cheer me on and join me in the journey. Thank you for helping me extend my dining room table and for faithfully praying. My parents taught me how to work hard and to fill my home with fun. When I say I am going to conquer a new challenge, they smile and say,

"Yes, you will!" Thank you for giving me confidence. My three children, William, Allie, and Katie, inspire me to keep learning and growing. They make me a better person.

Introduction

Within today's digital world, students intuitively acquire vast amounts of information at the touch of a screen or the tap of a keyboard. Learners in the information age long for more than activities that simply encourage the accumulation of additional knowledge. In fact, students come to class intuitively knowing how to gain a variety of information. Educational opportunities that transition students from consumers of information to creators of new learning experiences indelibly impact them in ways that transfer beyond the walls of the classroom.

Today's learners naturally and consistently consume, create, and publish content on their own time. Educators within the digital age leverage this creative potential when they allow and even encourage students to tap into their propensity for innovation in class. In an age in which far too few students understand how to effectively apply digital literacy or safety as they explore and generate content, today's educators hold the potential for far-reaching impact. Educators must learn to harness the enthusiasm students have for content creation (and particularly digital content creation) into everyday assessment opportunities. In doing so, they position themselves to enhance student engagement, motivation, and achievement in academic contexts.

Authentic Assessment in Action: An Everyday Guide for Bringing Learning to Life through Meaningful Assessment is designed to empower educators to provide highly impactful, consistently engaging, and unquestionably applicable learning opportunities for students.

Chapter 1 examines why authentic assessment matters through the perspective of today's learners. The world within and beyond school settings is portrayed through the eyes of Gen Z students, who constitute a group of learners with a practical eye towards professional pursuits and a vast familiarity with digital tools and resources.

As they brace for the immense responsibility of inheriting our planet, they also long for applicable educational experiences that will prepare them for the future. They anticipate a professional landscape that values creativity, collaboration, communication, critical thinking, global and digital citizenship, and genuine character. Through embarking on a reflective journey in the shoes of today's students, this chapter sets the stage for understanding learners' needs and interests to capture their motivation and engagement while addressing vital content standards.

Chapter 2 focuses more specifically on the types of assessments historically and typically featured in classrooms, as well as the implications on student learning. This chapter also explores varying assessment types, including teacher-centered (teachers exclusively identify, create, and evaluate) and student-centered (students create as a means of demonstrating their own learning). Formative and summative assessment means are considered as well.

Chapter 3 highlights the importance of allowing proven curricular frameworks and student learning outcomes (SLOs) to guide assessment design. This chapter offers practical strategies for formulating and articulating SLOs that will not only be meaningful to teachers and administrators, but even more importantly will be meaningful to students. Once key SLOs have been determined, they must be "marketed" to students in terms of how they apply to future professional endeavors. This chapter provides useful suggestions for sharing SLOs that support students in not only understanding but also ultimately embracing learning outcomes as their own.

Chapter 4 offers strategies for differentiating between assessment types and determining which type to utilize at various points in each instructional cycle. From formative to summative assessments, from teacher-centered to student-centered assessments (and every assessment type in between), this chapter empowers educators to design applicable, meaningful assessments, no matter the assessment type utilized.

Chapter 5 explores the profound impact that applicable and practical assessment measures render upon student learning experiences. As educators plan and implement authentic learning endeavors, students benefit from memorable and meaningful learning experiences that transfer to the world beyond the walls of the classroom. This chapter overviews an innovative formula for meaningful learning, namely "authentic issues + authentic audiences + authentic assessment = authentic learning experiences" (Alaniz, 2021). Chapter 5 outlines a plan for introducing students to real-world problems to solve, providing them with the opportunity to present solutions to various audiences, and designing assessment endeavors that apply to the everyday lives of learners.

Before delving deeply into integrating digital tools and resources within assessment opportunities, educators must thoughtfully ponder certain important considerations. Chapter 6 overviews the vital role educators play in guiding and empowering their students in safely and wisely leveraging digital tools and resources. Readers will also explore several crucial but often forgotten touchstones of our time, such as safety on social media and coping with COPPA (Children's Online Privacy and Protection Act) policies.

Chapter 7 comprises a summative overview of how learning is transformed when fostering an environment of meaningful assessment within school settings. As students achieve developmental milestones, their enthusiasm often becomes contagious, thus inspiring them to apply their learning beyond the walls of the classroom. This guidebook concludes with real-life success stories and testimonies involving authentic assessment, designed to inspire and inform readers in their journey to implement authentic assessment within their own professional settings. An investment in authentic assessment strategies holds the potential to profoundly and perpetually transform the culture of a campus—and even more so, the lives of today's students.

REFERENCES

Alaniz, K. (2021). *Collegial coaching: Mentoring for knowledge and skills that transfer to real-world applications.* Lanham, MD: Rowman & Littlefield Education.

Chapter 1

Starting with Why

Why Does Authentic Assessment Matter?

"How beautiful is youth!
How bright it gleams with its illusions, aspirations, dreams!
Book of beginnings, story without end,
Each maid a heroine, and each man a friend!"

—Henry Wadsworth Longfellow

In today's world, the word "youth" sparks a vast array of thoughts and emotions. While some individuals long for the days of bygone youth, others eagerly anticipate their advent into adulthood and the associated perceived freedoms not available to the young. While some envision youth as a world of wonder and freedom from the weight of responsibility, others long for the future, when they will grow old enough to acquire their dream job, purchase their dream home, and live out the life of their dreams. While individuals of a certain age spend fortunes to appear younger than they truly are, underage teenagers go to great lengths to appear older than their years.

Whether yearning for departed days or longing for the passage of time, everyone shares something in common: They were at one time a member of the newest generation—the generation being surveyed, studied, questioned, critiqued, and/or applauded. No matter the generation, individuals of each age group face certain generalizations, assumptions, and scrutiny.

As members of older generations attempt to understand those in their younger years, the temptation to marvel and criticize sometimes weighs heavier than the desire to seek first to understand. This compulsion represents a natural part of life, as one generation views the world from a different lens than the next. Albert Einstein once remarked, "The trouble with the younger generation is that they don't stay young for very long." For far too many, the passage of time happens far too quickly.

Yet, as older generations reflect upon their days of youth, it often becomes apparent that generational differences make more sense in light of the accelerating rate of change within today's world. In considering life in the 1800s and earlier, for example, it becomes clear that developments in society progressed much more slowly in bygone years. Centuries ago, individuals from even two or three generations were more likely to maintain comparable lifestyles. In more recent years, social and technological innovations have caused the lifestyles of individuals from one generation to the next to vary more dramatically than in the past.

As a result, a deficiency of intergenerational understanding has impacted today's educational institutions, corporations, nonprofit organizations, government agencies, social settings, and nearly every other area of society, including varying cyberspheres. This lack of intergenerational awareness and insight may manifest in sometimes subtle and oftentimes unsubtle ways, leading to unintended misunderstandings and negative consequences. In a digitally minded and globally interconnected world, these ramifications may easily span far beyond an isolated disagreement between a Gen X parent and Gen Z teenager.

One need only scan the comments provided in response to an even unintentionally generation-polarizing social media post. Disputes between members of various age groups may lead to hostile and overblown battles of the generations—battles that do not ultimately serve anyone involved. Now more than ever before, those who desire to impact and inspire today's youth most effectively do so through first seeking to understand the ways in which they think and operate. Yet, this requires a devotion of time, curiosity, study, and empathy on the part of those who desire to influence and encourage younger generations for the better. In many ways, these endeavors require significant paradigm shifts.

In fact, the generations represented within today's world vary so greatly from one to the next that they might be compared to unique cultures. Their perspectives, worldviews, backgrounds, and social mores dramatically and fundamentally differ. Without concerted efforts devoted to stretching across the cultural chasm, confusion and disagreements naturally result.

Even Socrates struggled to understand the newer generation and famously remarked,

> The children now love luxury; they have bad manners, contempt for authority; they show disrespect for elders and love chatter in place of exercise. Children are now tyrants, not the servants of their households. They no longer rise when elders enter the room. They contradict their parents, chatter before company, gobble up dainties at the table, cross their legs, and tyrannize their teachers.

By seeking first to understand, members of each generation position themselves to support others more effectively in leveraging strengths and moving forward, regardless of year of birth. Although the remainder of this chapter focuses most extensively upon Gen Z, the generation that represents the vast majority of learners within today's educational settings, a brief overview of the varying generations may support an understanding of the vast differences in viewpoints.

By exploring and reflecting upon unique characteristics among the various generations interacting within academic contexts, educators more effectively position themselves to reach and ultimately to impact those from different generations than their own. Parker and Igielnik (2020) of the Pew Research Center, along with Ryback (2016) of *Psychology Today*, outline some of the key overarching differences between those spanning from Boomers to Gen Z.

THE FLOWER CHILDREN: BABY BOOMERS (BORN 1946 TO 1964)

Baby Boomers represent the largest generational segment in the history of the United States, both from the standpoint of numbers as well as percentage of the population. Often considered the most influential generation, Baby Boomers were essential players in the civil rights movement, Woodstock, and the Vietnam War.

The term "Baby Boomer" resulted from a dramatic increase in rates of birth during the years following World War II. As soldiers returned home from the war and found themselves with additional time to create families, this ultimately resulted in a generational segment of more than 75 million individuals (or approximately twice the population of California).

As this generation did not come of age with access to innovative digital tools and resources, they grew up making phone calls from a landline and writing letters sent via "snail mail." Although they now utilize digital technologies more than ever before, they typically view such innovations from a productivity as opposed to connectivity standpoint, which represents a major differentiating factor between Baby Boomers and younger generations.

In pursuit of the "American Dream," many Baby Boomers began their careers in 9-to-5 professional roles. Their heightened focus upon job performance and advancement ultimately paved the way for a more workaholic view of success associated with corporate America, which is being restructured by younger generations, and particularly Millennials.

THE LOST GENERATION: GENERATION X (BORN 1965 TO 1980)

Known as the "sandwich" or "lost" generation, Generation X is wedged in between the two more prominently known and discussed generations, the Baby Boomers and the Millennials. Gen Xers have also been labeled as "latchkey kids" or the first "daycare" generation, as many were brought up by two working parents or by a single parent.

In an effort to concentrate on first improving themselves, many held off on finding a spouse and starting a family until reaching more advanced years than in previous generations. This generation delayed marriage and childbearing to focus on developing themselves first. As opposed to Baby Boomers in general, Gen Xers may focus a bit more on obtaining work-life balance, often veering from workaholism in favor of self-care and equilibrium between home/personal and professional spheres. This may be in response to enduring the broken homes resulting from workaholism among their parents.

THE MILLENNIALS (BORN 1981 TO 1996)

Millennials comprise the first generation to come of age in the new millennium, and they function as tech gurus who thrive as they innovate, invent start-ups, and work from nontraditional locations such as coffee shops, home offices, and shared workspaces. In some cases, members of this generation were raised by nonauthoritative parents who viewed their children as partners in parenting.

They are also known as digital pioneers in a number of areas, as Millennials were in some cases the first to rely upon digital tools and resources in ways that previous generations had not. Many Millennials find romance via dating websites and apps, and they may communicate far more easily and naturally through use of devices than through face-to-face conversations. They also tend to be more nomadic in nature, changing jobs, housing situations, relationship statuses, and other key lifestyle choices more frequently than many of their predecessors.

GENERATION Z (BORN IN 1997 AND THEREAFTER)

Although Millennials came of age amid the Great Recession, Gen Z was initially journeying along the path of inheriting a solid economy with historically low unemployment numbers. Yet, as the COVID-19 pandemic began wreaking havoc on the social, economic, and political environment of the United States and abroad, members of Gen Z began to face the realities of an unstable and unpredictable future.

Even in the initial stages of the pandemic, signs pointed to the fact that Gen Zers would be especially impacted by the COVID-19 crisis. In a study conducted by the Pew Research Center (2020), 50 percent of the oldest among the Gen Z population (ages 18 to 23 at the time) shared that either they themselves or an individual in their household endured a pay cut or job loss due to the pandemic.

This statistic represented a higher impact than experienced by those of the Millennial (40 percent), Gen X (36 percent), or Baby Boomer (25 percent) generations. Predictably, young workers were especially susceptible to the threat of job loss prior to the start of the pandemic, and their overrepresentation in more high-risk service-based industries only heightened the impact for Gen Zers throughout the pandemic.

Looking beyond the unusual time in history in which Gen Z is coming into their own, this generation differs from those who have come before it in a number of essential ways. For example, Gen Z represents greater ethnic and racial diversity than all other proceeding generations. Additionally, they are predicted to become the most well-educated generation in history. Not surprisingly, Gen Z is comprised of tech-savvy digital natives who may not have any recollection of the world prior to the advent of smartphones. They naturally and consistently consume, create, and publish content on their own time.

They represent the 9/11 generation, having come of age in a world in which violence may occur at any time and in any place, as well as a world in which smartphones and other recording devices make it possible to document and share such tragedies in real time. Technological advancements have paved the way for Gen Zers to witness devastating, life-altering events from an incredibly early age, opening their eyes to adversity that other generations may not have witnessed so vividly in their formative years.

They have grown up in educational settings in which lockdown drills are standard practice, and they have become accustomed to living in a state of preparedness for the worst. In their world, digital tools not only represent a means of remaining connected from a social standpoint, but these devices also symbolize necessary tools from a safety perspective. Their connectivity reflects their means of staying informed and connected should disaster strike, whether at school, in their workplaces, in social settings, or even at home.

Gen Z students constitute a group of learners with a practical eye toward professional pursuits and a vast familiarity with digital tools and resources. Over the course of their lifetime, they are expected to hold nearly 20 jobs, maintain a handful of careers, and occupy more than a dozen residences. This generation is seeking relevance and flexibility. As they brace for the immense responsibility of inheriting our planet, they also long for applicable educational experiences that will prepare them for the future.

They anticipate a professional landscape that values creativity, collaboration, communication, critical thinking, global and digital citizenship, and genuine character. In fact, they will find themselves within careers that have not yet been imagined. According to a 2018 study conducted by Dell Technologies and the Institute for the Future (IFTF), 85 percent of the jobs that will exist in 2030 are yet to be invented. Conducted in collaboration with 20 experts from around the world, this study sought to project into the future, predicting the ways in which emerging technologies (for example, artificial intelligence [AI] and the Internet of Things [IoT]) will alter humankind's methods of living and working in 2030.

The leaders surveyed within the study agree that the world is "on the verge of immense change" (p. 3). Among the study's key findings, the following insights shared by the study participants seem particularly applicable for today's educators and educational leaders: "Almost six in ten (56 percent) [of the leaders surveyed] say schools will need to teach how to learn rather than what to learn to prepare students for jobs that don't exist yet (corroborating IFTF's forecast that 85 percent of jobs that will exist in 2030 haven't been invented yet)" (p. 3).

Their insights apply not only to professional settings as they prepare to navigate the coming age, but they should also impact the ways in which educational settings seek to prepare today's students to meaningfully contribute and purposefully lead within tomorrow's workforce. Through embarking on a reflective journey in the shoes of today's students, educators who understand today's learners' needs and interests more effectively position themselves to capture their motivation and engagement while addressing vital content standards.

STARTING WITH WHY

In his inspirational book titled *Start with Why: How Great Leaders Inspire Everyone to Take Action*, Sinek (2011) shares that although most organizations can easily explain WHAT they do, and while some can also describe HOW they are unique or better, few can clearly communicate WHY they do what they do.

Considering the pragmatic nature of Gen Z individuals, they find greater motivation in pursuing endeavors in which the WHY is clearly identified. Whether in personal, professional, or educational settings, purposeful pursuits inspire lasting growth from today's students, as well as greater buy-in—even from those who are at first hesitant to engage in endeavors that stretch them beyond their comfort zones. They desire to clearly identify the practical reasons for pursuing a destination before starting the journey.

BRIDGING THE GREAT DIVIDE: ADDRESSING EDUCATIONAL NEEDS AND EXPECTATIONS BETWEEN GENERATIONS

Within today's digital world, students intuitively acquire vast amounts of information at the touch of a screen or the tap of a keyboard. Learners in the information age long for more than activities that simply encourage the accumulation of additional knowledge. In fact, students come to class intuitively knowing how to gain a variety of information. Educational opportunities that transition students from consumers of information to creators of new learning experiences indelibly impact them in ways that transfer beyond the walls of the classroom.

Educators within the digital age leverage this creative potential when they allow and even encourage students to tap into their propensity for innovation in class. In an age in which far too few students understand how to effectively apply digital literacy or safety as they explore and generate content, today's educators hold the potential for far-reaching impact. They must learn to harness the enthusiasm students have for content creation (and particularly digital content creation) into everyday assessment opportunities. In doing so, they position themselves to enhance student engagement, motivation, and achievement in academic contexts.

BEGINNING WITH THE END IN MIND

In his enduring, frequently quoted book *The 7 Habits of Highly Effective People: Restoring the Character Ethic*, Covey (1989) outlines life principles that naturally translate to countless personal and professional endeavors. One of these principles, Habit 2, highlights the importance of beginning with the end in mind. Covey once remarked, "To begin with the end in mind means to start with a clear understanding of your destination. It means to know where you're going so that you better understand where you are now and so that the steps you take are always in the right direction."

The coming chapters highlight the importance of "beginning with the end in mind" and "starting with WHY" as foundational principles in designing impactful authentic assessment endeavors.

ESSENTIAL IDEAS TO REMEMBER

In order to profoundly impact today's learners, effective educators and educational leaders seek to understand the world through the lens of their students. Gen Z learners represent a group of students with a practical eye toward professional pursuits and a vast familiarity with digital tools and resources. As they prepare to take on the enormous responsibility of inheriting the earth, they also long for applicable educational experiences that will prepare them for the future.

The professional landscape they will enter values creativity, collaboration, communication, critical thinking, global and digital citizenship, and genuine character. Through embarking on a reflective journey in the shoes of today's students, educators and educational leaders better position themselves to meet learners' needs and interests, ultimately capturing their motivation and engagement while addressing vital content standards.

REFERENCES

Covey, S. R. (1989). *The 7 habits of highly effective people: Restoring the character ethic.* New York: Free Press.

Dell Technologies (2018). *Realizing 2030: A divided vision of the future.* https://bit.ly/2FvF1yi

Parker, K., & Igielnik, R. (2020, May 14). On the cusp of adulthood and facing an uncertain future: What we know about Gen Z so far. Pew Research Center. https://www.pewresearch.org/social-trends/2020/05/14/on-the-cusp

-of-adulthood-and-facing-an-uncertain-future-what-we-know-about-gen-z-so-far-2/

Pew Research Center (2020, March 26). Worries about Coronavirus surge, as most Americans expect a recession—or worse. Pew Research Center. https://www.pewresearch.org/politics/2020/03/26/worries-about-coronavirus-surge-as-most-americans-expect-a-recession-or-worse/

Ryback, R. (2016, February 22). From Baby Boomers to Gen Z: A detailed look at the characteristics of each generation. *Psychology Today*. https://www.psychologytoday.com/us/blog/the-truisms-wellness/201602/baby-boomers-generation-z

Sinek, S. (2011). *Start with why*. Harlow, England: Penguin Books.

Chapter 2

Considering Key Findings
What Does the Research Say?

"Assessment is today's means of modifying tomorrow's instruction."

— Carol Ann Tomlinson

With the arrival of the twentieth century, public schools implemented a variety of academic "innovations" that aligned with the prominent educational theories of the time. Such developments highlighted the value of efficiency, and overarching goals included mass-producing students capable of basic reading, writing, and computing. As explained within the book *How People Learn* (National Academies of Sciences, Engineering, and Medicine, 2000):

> In the early 1900s, the challenge of providing mass education was seen by many as analogous to mass production in factories. School administrators were eager to make use of the "scientific" organization of factories to structure efficient classrooms. Children were regarded as raw materials to be efficiently processed by technical workers (the teachers) to reach the end product (Bennett & LeCompte, 1990; Callahan, 1962; Kliebard, 1975). This approach attempted to sort the raw materials (the children) so that they could be treated somewhat as an assembly line. Teachers were viewed as workers whose job was to carry out directives from their superiors—the efficiency experts of schooling (administrators and researchers). (p. 132)

Moreover, these ideals indelibly impacted assessment methods, paving the way for the advent of standardized testing:

The emulation of factory efficiency fostered the development of standardized tests for measurement of the "product," of clerical work by teachers to keep records of costs and progress (often at the expense of teaching), and of "management" of teaching by central district authorities who had little knowledge of educational practice or philosophy (Callahan, 1962). In short, the factory model affected the design of curriculum, instruction, and assessment in schools. (National Academies of Sciences, Engineering, and Medicine, 2000, p. 132)

Yet, in the present digital age, the knowledge and skills needed for success in innovative professional contexts differ greatly than those sought more than a century ago. More so than ever before, professional environments consistently morph as technological developments are made, prompting the need for a steady reskilling of workers and a consistently changing job market. In an ever-changing professional landscape, today's educators are tasked with the challenge of preparing their students for future opportunities that may not yet exist.

Although it might be impossible to predict exactly what types of occupations students will pursue in the future, educators can empower their students to develop the skills needed to be successful in any job—even those that have not yet been invented. Rather than relying on a mass-production, standardized mindset, future-focused curricular and instructional design equips students with skills that will be applicable for life beyond school settings. These include the "Six C's" of learning in the digital age, which will be highlighted throughout forthcoming chapters and were originally presented within a white paper by Fullan and Scott (2014, pp. 6–7):

- Character: "Qualities of the individual essential for being personally effective in a complex world, including grit, tenacity, perseverance, resilience, reliability, and honesty"
- Citizenship: "Thinking like global citizens, considering global issues based on a deep understanding of diverse values with genuine interest in engaging with others to solve complex problems that impact human and environmental sustainability"
- Collaboration: "The capacity to work interdependently and synergistically in teams with strong interpersonal and team-related skills including effective management of team dynamics, making

substantive decisions together, and learning from and contributing to the learning of others"
- Communication: "Mastery of three fluencies: digital, writing, and speaking tailored for a range of audiences"
- Creativity: "Having an 'entrepreneurial eye' for economic and social opportunities, asking the right questions to generate novel ideas, and demonstrating leadership to pursue those ideas into practice"
- Critical Thinking: "Critically evaluating information and arguments, seeing patterns and connections, construction meaningful knowledge and applying it in the real world"

COMPARING AND CONTRASTING FORMATIVE AND SUMMATIVE ASSESSMENTS

Students in today's educational settings need to be empowered to build upon their current knowledge, so they are ultimately prepared to make wise decisions in the future, even in the face of ambiguity. Assessment practices play a vital role in empowering students in these types of future-focused learning endeavors. In his book *Classroom Assessment and Grading That Work*, Marzano (2006) summarized research on the history of classroom assessment. His findings revealed that feedback from academic assessments should provide students with a clear picture of their progress, encourage students to learn, be formative in nature, and be frequent.

By giving students a clear picture of their progress and how to improve, students are able to approach their learning as collaborators rather than passive audience members. With formative assessment, students should feel encouraged to learn rather than encouraged to "close the book" on this chapter of learning. When students see the goal as learning rather than achieving a particular grade, they are more likely to recall important information and actively engage in ongoing learning.

One often-used explanation of the difference between formative and summative assessment is that formative assessment might be likened to visiting the doctor for a physical while summative assessment represents the autopsy. Formative assessment should inform an educator's understanding of how students are able to understand and apply student learning outcomes. Such assessments should be engaging, frequent, and low stakes. As reiterated in Greenstein's (2010) book *What Teachers Really Need to Know about Formative Assessment*, formative assessment is *for* learning and used to improve learning.

Tables 2.1 and 2.2, developed by the Center for Teaching and Learning Excellence at Saint Leo University (2022), outline the two assessment types, as well as offer a variety of examples of formative and summative assessments.

Due to the nature of formative assessments, they are not intended to require a substantial investment of time. A one-minute paper entails students spending one minute writing down all they learned during a previous lesson. A fist-to-five involves learners holding up a hand with a fist representing a lack of understanding, five fingers representing self-reported mastery of the material, and a number in between representing various degrees of understanding. Other examples of formative assessment can be found at the following websites:

- Classcraft's 62 Ways to Check for Understanding: https://www.classcraft.com/blog/ways-to-check-for-understanding/

Figure 2.1. Classcraft's 62 Ways to Check for Understanding

- Edutopia's 53 Ways to Check for Understanding: https://ceedar.education.ufl.edu/wp-content/uploads/2021/07/edutopia-finley-53-ways-to-check-understanding-2016.pdf

Figure 2.2. Edutopia's 53 Ways to Check for Understanding

Table 2.1.

Formative Assessment	Summative Assessment
Assessment **for** learning	Assessment **of** learning
Purpose: to provide feedback/information to:	Purpose: to evaluate student learning or mastery at the end of a chapter, unit, or course
a. improve/adjust instruction, and/or	
b. provide information to students to foster growth	
Focuses on process	Focuses on product
Monitors learning	Assesses learning
Occurs during instructional process	Occurs at end of instructional process
Informal or formal	Formal
Low stakes/low point value	High stakes/high point value
Results used to provide feedback to support student growth or inform teacher practice	Results used to provide grades
Provides opportunities to improve performance	No opportunity to change result/grade

Table 2.2.

Formative Assessments Examples	Summative Assessments Examples
Quizzes	End-of-chapter test
Exit tickets	End-of-unit test
Polling in class, surveys	End-of-course exam
One-minute paper	Midterm exam
Homework or classwork	Final project or paper
Infographics, charts, diagrams	Portfolio
Summary or bullet points of reading or lecture	Certification exams
Talking or discussion	
Reflective activities	
Socratic seminar	
Self-assessment	
Peer feedback/review	

TEACHER-CREATED VERSUS STUDENT-CREATED ASSESSMENTS

In a teacher-centered assessment model, teachers exclusively identify, create, and evaluate. Other than taking an assessment, students have no involvement in the assessment process, and likely, little involvement in the learning process. In a student-centered assessment model, students create as a means of demonstrating their own learning. In this model, students have greater ownership in their learning and academic progress. When students are active participants in assessment, they are able to monitor their own learning and learning gaps. One way to shift from teacher-centered to student-centered assessment is by understanding how the brain receives, retains, and retrieves information.

Sprenger (2018) wrote that educators need to follow seven clear steps to help students remember what they have learned. Step one in this process is "Reach and Teach," meaning that the teacher must find a way to engage the students in the learning process.

Step two is "Reflect." During this stage, students should be given the opportunity to make connections in the material being learned. "By manipulating the new information in working memory, they connect it with older, long-term memories" (Sprenger, 2018). This stage is a perfect time for a formative assessment.

The third step, "Recode," allows students the opportunity to restate information in their own words. Again, this could be an example of formative assessment. By allowing students to create, teach someone else, or generate their own material, they can start the process of transferring knowledge from working memory to long-term memory.

Step four, "Reinforce," allows educators to offer feedback from the formative assessment stages. Sprenger states that the feedback could be motivational, informational, and developmental. This feedback makes it possible for the learner and the teacher to communicate about what is known and what still needs to be learned.

Steps five and six are unique but connected. Step five is the "Rehearse" stage, while step six is the "Review" stage. Rehearsing helps create networks of neurons throughout the brain to help in the process of moving to permanent memory. Reviewing helps retrieve the material once it has made the transfer to permanent memory. Through providing opportunities for students to review, neural networks will be strengthened and retrieval will become easier. Without proper review, it is not likely the learned material will be retained in long-term memory. Therefore, cramming for a test may help in the short term but not in the long term.

The final step of the process of teaching so that students will remember is to aid students in retrieving the information. At this stage, teaching, formative assessment with reflection, practice, and review have taken place. By helping students practice retrieval of learned material, summative assessment scores will likely indicate higher student achievement.

Authentic assessment, which is the focus of the remainder of the book, challenges educators and their students to make connections to the real world. Problem-solving endeavors that apply to everyday life require students to apply the material learned. Traditional forced-answer assessments (such as those involving multiple choice) do not necessarily encourage students to apply, create, or use material learned. Authentic assessment bridges that gap.

Table 2.3, developed by the Center for Innovative Teaching and Learning at Indiana University Bloomington (2022), highlights key differences between traditional and authentic assessment methods.

Frequent, applicable assessment methods that inform both educators and their students will more effectively support the long-term learning that is needed for this generation's success in the future.

ESSENTIAL IDEAS TO REMEMBER

Considering today's ever-changing professional landscape, the process of developing basic numeracy, literacy, and content knowledge is not enough to prepare learners for the future they will face beyond their schooling years. Preparation for the future begins today. In order for students to be capable of navigating the complex world they will inherit, they must be able to create successfully, think critically, communicate effectively, collaborate skillfully, and consistently demonstrate citizenship and character.

Rather than simply recalling what they have memorized for a quiz or test, they must be able to apply the knowledge and skills they have acquired to future academic, professional, and personal endeavors. This is what authentic assessment is all about. The remainder of this book delves into practical approaches for meaningfully preparing students

Table 2.3.

Typical Tests	Authentic Tasks	Indicators of Authenticity
Require correct responses	Require a high-quality product or performance and a justification of the solutions to problems encountered	Correctness is not the only criterion; students must be able to justify their answers.
Must be unknown to the student in advance to be valid	Should be known in advance to students as much as possible	The tasks and standards for judgment should be known or predictable.
Are disconnected from real-world contexts and constraints	Are tied to real-world contexts and constraints; require the student to "do" the subject	The context and constraints of the task are like those encountered by practitioners in the discipline.
Contain items that isolate particular skills or facts	Are integrated challenges in which a range of skills and knowledge must be used in coordination	The task is multifaceted and complex, even if there is a right answer.
Include easily scored items	Involve complex tasks for which there may be no right answer and that may not be easily scored	The validity of the assessment is not sacrificed in favor of reliable scoring.
Are "one shot"; students get one chance to show their learning	Are iterative; contain recurring tasks	Students may use particular knowledge or skills in several different ways or contexts.
Provide a score	Provide usable diagnostic information about students' skills and knowledge	The assessment is designed to improve future performance, and students are important "consumers" of such information.

for the future through authentic assessment methods that can be implemented today.

REFERENCES

Bennett, K. P., & LeCompte, M. D. (1990). *The way schools work: A sociological analysis of education.* New York: Longman.

Callahan, R. E. (1962). *Education and the cult of efficiency.* Chicago: University of Chicago Press.

Fullan, M., & Scott, G. (2014). *New pedagogies for deep learning whitepaper: Education PLUS*. Seattle, WA: Collaborative Impact SPC.

Greenstein, L. (2010). *What teachers really need to know about formative assessment*. Alexandria, VA: Association for Supervision and Curriculum Development.

Indiana University Bloomington. (2022). *Authentic assessment*. Center for Innovative Teaching and Learning. https://citl.indiana.edu/teaching-resources/assessing-student-learning/authentic-assessment/index.html

Kliebard, H. M. (1975). Metaphorical roots of curriculum design. In *Curriculum Theorizing: The Reconceptualists*, W. Pinar, ed. Berkeley: McCutchan.

Marzano, R. J., & Association for Supervision and Curriculum Development. (2006). *Classroom assessment and grading that work*. Alexandria, VA: Association for Supervision and Curriculum Development.

National Academies of Sciences, Engineering, and Medicine. (2000). *How people learn: Brain, mind, experience, and school: Expanded edition*. Washington, DC: The National Academies Press. https://doi.org/10.17226/9853

Saint Leo University. (2022). *Formative and summative assessment*. Center for Teaching and Learning Excellence. https://faculty.saintleo.edu/teaching/assessment/formativesummativeassessment

Sprenger, M. (2018). *How to teach so students remember*. Alexandria, VA: Association for Supervision and Curriculum Development.

Thomas, L. (2019, April 26). *7 smart, fast ways to do formative assessment*. Edutopia. Retrieved July 13, 2022, from https://www.edutopia.org/article/7-smart-fast-ways-do-formative-assessment

Chapter 3

Beginning with the End in Mind

How Do Curricular Frameworks and Student Learning Outcomes Impact Assessment?

> *"To begin with the end in mind means to start with a clear understanding of your destination. It means to know where you're going so that you better understand where you are now and so that the steps you take are always in the right direction."*
>
> —Stephen R. Covey (1989)

In his classic, frequently referenced book *The 7 Habits of Highly Effective People: Restoring the Character Ethic*, Covey (1989) outlines principles for life that apply to innumerable personal and professional endeavors. Among these principles, Habit 2 points to the value of beginning with the end in mind. This particular habit significantly impacts assessment endeavors, specifically when considering the creation of student learning outcomes (SLOs).

Insightful, forward-thinking individuals plan new adventures in life by first contemplating the ultimate destination. Just as it would be unwise to begin packing for a journey without considering the journey's end, it would be ill-advised to embark upon teaching a unit or lesson without considering key SLOs.

In the words of Covey (1989), "We may be very busy, we may be very 'efficient,' but we will also be truly 'effective' only when we begin with the end in mind." In a mile-a-minute culture in which many individuals and organizations seek to move through to-do's and next steps at breakneck speed, the power of reflection (especially prior to the start of a new endeavor) is often overlooked. With technology at the world's fingertips, few can resist the temptation to sit at a redlight without connecting to social media or scrolling.

Concerning the process of reflection, Aristotle remarked, "It is the mark of an educated mind to be able to entertain a thought without accepting it." Yogi Berra, a notable American baseball star also known for his clever quotes, echoed these sentiments with the following sage advice: "If you don't know where you're going, you'll end up someplace else."

In the book *Collegial Coaching: Mentoring for Knowledge and Skills That Transfer to Real-World Applications* (Alaniz, 2021), the correlation between beginning with the end in mind and Sinek's (2011) now renowned tenet "start with why" is overviewed in relation to educator professional development. These principles also include many parallels as they relate to assessment design. In his inspiring book *Start with Why: How Great Leaders Inspire Everyone to Take Action*, Sinek (2011) maintains that even though countless organizations can clearly describe WHAT they do, and while some organizations can also explain HOW they are exceptional or outstanding, very few organizations effectively convey WHY they exist.

Sinek (2011) explains,

> Knowing your WHY is not the only way to be successful, but it is the only way to maintain a lasting success and have a greater blend of innovation and flexibility. When a WHY goes fuzzy, it becomes much more difficult to maintain the growth, loyalty and inspiration that helped drive the original success. By difficult, I mean that manipulation rather than inspiration fast becomes the strategy of choice to motivate behavior. This is effective in the short term but comes at a high cost in the long term. (p. 50)

Like leaders within any professional context, educators more consistently and effectively inspire long-term success in student learning and intrinsic motivation among learners as they keep the WHY at the forefront of instructional endeavors. The most efficacious educators not only remain mindful of the WHY for each new learning endeavor, but they also articulate this WHY consistently—and even more importantly, encourage students to formulate and articulate their own WHY(s).

Through this process, they foster a setting in which sustained buy-in and growth from students—even reluctant or seemingly unmotivated learners—occur more naturally and frequently. When students connect a personally valued WHY to their learning, they will be more likely to engage with learning materials, the teacher, and their peers. Excellent educators clearly pinpoint and articulate the ultimate destination before beginning any new instructional journey, and the upcoming chapters build upon research and experiences that provide a strong case for the WHY behind purposeful authentic assessment endeavors.

Educators who seek to design and implement each unit and lesson with the end in mind while keeping the WHY at the forefront more effectively foster genuine engagement from students, as well as truly purposeful, applicable learning experiences. According to Alaniz (2021),

> When educators develop a clear vision for where students should arrive prior to commencing new learning journeys, the likelihood of students taking action to reach this destination increases significantly. Unfortunately, far too many educational systems and teachers within them pack each day with busy work that fails to bring students closer to the overarching goals and corresponding objectives. Many educators unknowingly become so caught up in daily "to do's" that they have little time remaining to think about the purpose behind their work or the tasks on which their students are laboring away each day. In cases such as this, teachers and their students might begin to feel as though they are travelling down a path without purpose; journeys without the WHY eventually begin to seem murky and arduous. (p. 72)

Prior to creating and implementing any new instructional unit or lesson, the most effective educators devote time and careful reflection to considering and answering questions such as those listed below (Alaniz, 2021, pp. 72–73):

- Why are you teaching this unit?
- Why are you passionate about this content?
- Beyond answers such as, "This content is mandated by the state or district," why is this unit or lesson important for students to learn?

- Why should students care about learning this content?
- What overarching goals should students obtain through this unit?
- What corresponding objectives should students grasp through this unit?
- What artifacts of learning might students create to demonstrate that they have mastered the knowledge and skills addressed within these goals and objectives?

As educators reflect upon these questions and grasp a clear vision for the WHY associated with the upcoming journey and the destination learners will be progressing toward, they and their students become more effectively equipped to traverse the road ahead. The frameworks that "begin with the end in mind" and "start with why" offer meaning and power in curriculum mapping and instructional undertakings.

A first step in purposeful planning involves the selection of an appropriate, helpful curricular design model. While quite a few curricular development frameworks exist, those overviewed in this chapter have proved to be incredibly effective over time through a variety of research studies and when applied in diverse educational settings.

THE UNDERSTANDING BY DESIGN FRAMEWORK

Developed by Jay McTighe and Grant Wiggins (2012), the Understanding by Design framework provides educators with a recognized model of establishing effective teaching and learning procedures. The following represent key principles associated with this model:

1. When educators intentionally reflect upon curricular planning processes, improved learning outcomes result.
2. In curricular design and instructional endeavors, emphasis should be upon the advancement and extension of students' understanding of content, as well as upon learners' ability to transfer attained knowledge and skills to future pursuits.
3. When students engage in experiences that allow them to independently make sense of new learning, their new understandings are revealed. This happens as they are provided opportunities to apply

their newly acquired knowledge and skills in everyday, authentic applications.
4. Effective curricular planning encompasses the "backward design" framework, which features the following elements:
   a. Educators should first pinpoint desired results for their students. Throughout this identification phase, foundational questions such as the following should be reflected upon: "Ultimately, what should learners know and be able to do? Along these lines, what central standards need to be addressed?"
   b. Educators should also create a set of learning goals (student learning outcomes) to journey toward. This process entails pinpointing essential enduring understandings that students will continue to access and build upon long after the unit or lesson has come to an end.
   c. Educators must also identify evidence of learning that students should ultimately be able to demonstrate. Each evidence of learning should include specified strategies for gauging the extent to which learners have grasped necessary knowledge and skills.
   d. Finally, a learning plan must be established. This plan should empower and encourage educators and their students to begin with the end in mind. This plan should be considered a road map or guide toward reaching the desired destination, or goals established prior to the start of the journey.

When executed successfully, the Understanding by Design framework helps educators and their students avoid common obstacles to meaningful learning that may otherwise be found in classroom contexts. For example, this framework discourages them from relying upon the textbook(s) as the curricular guide rather than simply viewing textbooks as curricular resources. Furthermore, it prevents activity-driven learning endeavors void of purpose and clearly defined educational priorities. The Understanding by Design framework ultimately supports educators in placing first things first and keeping the end in mind. This classic method of curricular planning provides a solid guide for learner-centered, purposeful, applicable educational endeavors.

THE UNIVERSAL DESIGN FOR LEARNING (UDL) MODEL

Universal Design for Learning (UDL) represents an alternate curricular planning strategy that emphasizes flexibility and variety in the delivery of content as well as in assessment practices. In 2008, the Higher Education Opportunity Act (HEOA) was passed with solid bipartisan support, thereby forming a legislative definition for UDL.

Supported by widespread research, UDL represents an important framework for guiding educational pursuits that highlights a number of essential goals. In particular, it provides flexible strategies for presenting content in an academic setting. Furthermore, this framework offers a variety of options for engaging learners, soliciting responses from students, and encouraging them to demonstrate newly acquired knowledge and skills.

The UDL framework lessens instructional barriers, enabling educators to offer helpful accommodations while providing rigorous learning experiences through high expectations for every student. This model supports educators in providing differentiated content representation. UDL encourages educators to incorporate student choice in their demonstrations of learning, including tangible products as well as communicative actions. Additionally, the UDL framework promotes multiple strategies for student engagement; each strategy is designed to promote learners' curiosity, perseverance, and self-regulation.

UDL impacts the ways in which educators think about factors preventing students from learning. Rather than viewing student learning difficulties in terms of what needs to change about the students, UDL focuses upon the learning environment. This environment may entail certain barriers to learning, such as the design of student learning outcomes, assessment measures, instructional strategies, and learning resources. UDL provides educators with a paradigm and framework for reducing barriers to learning. The primary means of accomplishing this goal is through cultivating a learning environment in which all students can flexibly achieve learning outcomes.

BLOOM'S TAXONOMY

Meaningful curricular planning endeavors hinge on the knowledge and skills students will eventually make use of in real-world contexts, as well as strategies for accomplishing set student learning outcomes. A classic foundation for curricular development, Bloom's Taxonomy focuses upon actions students use to convey their understanding and capacity to apply learned content in real-life settings.

Bloom's Taxonomy, designed by Dr. Benjamin Bloom in 1956, offers a clear-cut framework for classifying learning outcomes educators may develop for their students. This method was created to be integrated throughout instructional cycles as learners grasp content in progressively complex ways. Identifying essential, varied learning goals and objectives parallels the process of pinpointing desired results through the Understanding by Design framework.

This is the point at which educators must begin with the end in mind, deciding what students should ultimately know and be able to do. Effective instructional endeavors empower students to transition from lower levels within the taxonomy to higher levels, ultimately encompassing authentic learning of essential content.

The levels are as follows:

- Remembering: recalling basic facts, concepts, and answers
- Understanding: comparing, interpreting, or providing descriptions and key ideas
- Applying: solving problems in new situations by using acquired facts, techniques, and rules pertaining to the content at hand
- Analyzing: formulating inferences and generalizations about the topic while relating it to previously learned content
- Evaluating: validating ideas, making judgments, and defending perspectives based on criteria and evidence pertaining to content
- Creating: restructuring content into a novel pattern or framework

Bloom's Taxonomy aligns with the Understanding by Design framework in that it focuses upon verbs describing what students ultimately need to be able to do as a means of demonstrating new knowledge or skills learned. The verbs within the taxonomy correspond with desired evidence, or actionable student learning outcomes. The taxonomy also provides a framework through which educators can decipher whether student learning outcomes tap into higher-order skills or reside solely in the lower levels of Bloom's, focusing on remembering and understanding. Such practices ultimately inhibit students from developing high-level skills such as evaluating and creating.

DESIGNING ACTIONABLE, PURPOSEFUL STUDENT LEARNING OUTCOMES

Through considering the ways in which Bloom's Taxonomy applies to curricular frameworks such as Understanding by Design or the Universal Design for Learning, educators better position their students to transition from functioning as consumers of information to creators of new learning experiences. American businessman Louis V. Gerstner Jr. remarked, "People don't do what you expect but what you inspect." This adage is true within educational settings as well. By beginning with the end in mind and starting with WHY, educators better prepare themselves to write meaningful, measurable SLOs.

An actionable, purposeful student learning outcome entails the inclusion of three key factors:

1. Behavior: By utilizing action verbs from the applicable level(s) of Bloom's Taxonomy, educators can easily describe the desired behavior that will provide evidence of learning. Verbs such as "understand" or "comprehend" are not actionable; they cannot be demonstrated in a way that others can witness. Thus, for the purpose of developing actionable, purposeful SLOs, such verbs should be avoided. The following examples include a description of desired behaviors:

    - Recall the definitions
    - Identify the key concepts
    - Describe the steps
    - Compare and contrast the theories
    - Justify the central argument of
    - Construct a plan of action
    - Create a professional portfolio

2. Conditions: In addition to an actionable behavior, effective SLOs also include information regarding the conditions under which the identified behavior will be demonstrated. This segment of the SLO incorporates tools or resources the students will utilize in demonstrating their learning as well. The following are examples of SLO conditions:

- Given a protractor and five distinct angles
- Given the outline of a speech
- Given a description of three different variables
- Given the following scenario

3. Standard: The final component of an effective SLO entails an explanation of the standard or criteria that will be utilized as a means of evaluating success. This segment of the outcome describes to what extent the learner must perform to demonstrate achievement of the SLO. The following is a list of standard examples:

- At least 85 percent of
- Accurately demonstrates the principles of
- Comprehensively addresses each of the questions
- Includes a description of at least 500 words

Actionable, purposeful student learning outcomes include the three aforementioned facets. The following represent examples of complete SLOs, including behaviors, conditions, and standards.

- Given the following scenario (**condition**), illustrate (**behavior**) the five styles of effective communication in the workplace through specific examples of each (**standard**).
- Given a sample web page (**condition**), accurately apply (**behavior**) HTML coding principles (**standard**) to create (**behavior**) a new table summarizing the key content presented on the page (**standard**).
- Given the six principles of design (**condition**), create (**behavior**) an infographic that effectively illustrates applications of each principle in an original format (**standard**).

While behaviors, conditions, and standards represent key components of designing actionable student leaning outcomes, even the most effectively written SLOs lack influence unless accompanied by the WHY. Students naturally lack motivation to learn if they cannot understand or articulate why their learning matters. When desired SLOs are presented hand in hand with discussion regarding why they matter in everyday life, learners more naturally feel inspired to engage and persist in achieving set outcomes. Upcoming chapters will incorporate strategies for ensuring the WHY is at the forefront as SLOs are presented and learners endeavor toward accomplishing them.

ESSENTIAL IDEAS TO REMEMBER

Effective curricular planning might understandably seem somewhat overwhelming for today's educators, especially in a climate in which many feel pressured to cram as much content as possible into each new lesson. It can seem challenging to decipher which educational endeavors are worth pursuing and how implementation should happen.

As educators start with WHY, allowing end goals, or student learning outcomes founded in real-world applicability, to drive instructional endeavors, learning becomes more meaningful. By reflecting upon the final destination and encouraging students to do the same, educators more effectively prepare their students for a purposeful and impactful journey to come. Rather than feeling as though they are along for the ride, as students are empowered to understand and articulate their WHY, they become active participants in the great adventure of learning—an adventure they will not easily forget.

REFERENCES

Alaniz, K. (2021). *Collegial coaching: Mentoring for knowledge and skills that transfer to real-world applications.* Lanham, MD: Rowman & Littlefield Education.

Covey, S. R. (1989). *The 7 habits of highly effective people: Restoring the character ethic.* New York: Free Press.

McTighe, J., & Wiggins, G. (2012). The Understanding by Design framework. *White Paper*. Alexandria, VA: ASCD. http://www.ascd.org/ASCD/pdf/siteASCD/publications/UbD_WhitePaper0312.pdf

Sinek, S. (2011). *Start with why*. Harlow, England: Penguin Books.

Wiggins, G., & McTighe, J. (2005). *Understanding by design* (2nd edition). Upper Saddle River, NJ: Pearson/Merrill Education/ASCD. ISBN: 0-205-57860-8

Chapter 4

Exploring Assessments, Assessments, and More Assessments

Which Assessment Type Should Be Used When?

> *"In an effective classroom, students should not only know what they are doing. They should also know why and how."*
>
> —Harry Wong

Today's educators find themselves facing snowballing demands for accountability, such as high-stakes testing, ever more rigorous regulations, and heightened curricular standards. With this being the case, they may naturally feel as though there is little margin for creating innovative assessment endeavors. For educators lacking time and in some cases depleted of energy to try new instructional strategies, out-of-the-box assessment design might seem a low priority, if not an impossibility.

Yet, by proactively investing in planning purposeful assessment strategies, educators ultimately may find that less time is needed for reactive endeavors such as backtracking through past lessons and reteaching already covered content. Through utilizing an authentic approach to planning formative and summative assessments—complete with rubrics to gauge student learning—educators and learners more successfully remain on track toward achieving set student learning outcomes. This chapter highlights applicable strategies to support educators in ensuring that student assessment endeavors actually accomplish what they are intended to accomplish.

As addressed in depth in chapter 3, successful curricular and instructional planning involves beginning with the end in mind. As described by Wilson, Alaniz, and Sikora (2016), this process may be likened to physical journeys in life:

> Just as travelers embark on journeys with a vision for the final destination as their driving focus, effective educators map curriculum with a clear picture of what students should ultimately know or be able to do at the forefront of their minds. Such teachers design authentic assessment pieces in light of predetermined standards, thus confirming that these assessments will ultimately gauge the extent to which students have achieved desired learning outcomes. (p. 105)

The most successful educational journeys involve set criteria for measuring evidence of acquired knowledge and skills—and discussing those assessment measures with students even before the start of the journey. This allows learners to know exactly what to expect along the way, and it provides them with feasible outcomes to work toward achieving. Steve Jobs once remarked, "If you are working on something exciting that you really care about, you don't have to be pushed. The vision pulls you." Learners should not simply be given directions for completing the next activity, one activity at a time. Instead, they should be empowered to operate as collaborators in casting a vision and accomplishing outcomes related to that vision.

Before any new unit or lesson begins, it is essential that educators discuss the WHY for each upcoming learning adventure and support their students in grasping the vision. Students should not only understand the purpose of every forthcoming learning endeavor, but they should also be able to clearly articulate this purpose. It is never too early to begin incorporating this crucial component of authentic learning. Even students within early childhood classrooms can grasp and appreciate the WHY, if learning is directly related to everyday life.

Thinking back on their time spent in classroom settings as students, adults beyond their schooling years seldom remember information they were expected to "cram" for an exam. Yet, most adults can readily recall a hands-on lesson conducted in a classroom context that somehow applied to everyday life.

Why is this the case? Human beings naturally crave experiences that provide meaning—experiences that directly apply to their authentic life experiences. They more easily internalize and recall learning endeavors associated with a sense of purpose. Neurologist and former teacher Judy Willis (2008) points to the need for personal relevance and emotional engagement to aid in memory storage. Actor Hank Azaria once commented, "There's no experience like on-the-job training." Working professionals often acknowledge that most of the learning needed for their profession has occurred on the job. Could it be that this is the case at least partially because their prior educational experiences did not transfer to professional contexts?

When students find themselves unable to decipher how their learning in the classroom applies to their personal and future professional contexts, they may naturally lack the intrinsic motivation to learn. In situations involving "teaching to the test" rather than appealing to learners' engagement in real-life experiences, some students may be extrinsically driven to earn a certain grade. Yet, their curiosity and passion for learning will ultimately remain unkindled. Sir Winston Churchill observed, "Where my reason, imagination, or interest were not engaged, I would not or could not learn." This is the case for countless individuals, and particularly today's students.

AN ARRAY OF ASSESSMENT FORMATS

The *Glossary of Education Reform* (Abbott, 2015) defines assessment as "the wide variety of methods or tools that educators use to evaluate, measure, and document the academic readiness, learning progress, skill acquisition, or educational needs of students." Among these tools, standardized assessment practices occupy a progressively more dominant role in influencing instructional practices in educational contexts. Designed by testing companies to collect data in relation to achievement among substantial populations of learners, standardized assessments most often incorporate multiple-choice formats.

Among the varied assessment types, standards-based assessments epitomize a cornerstone of today's educational systems. Designed to measure students' knowledge and skills associated with select learning standards, these assessments may be created by states, school districts, or individual schools. They purpose to evaluate proficiency levels of learners and, if utilized as intended, serve to guide educators' instructional practices. When established and/or utilized in a school context or district setting, such assessment instruments may be labeled "common assessments." In these cases, they should be constructed, delivered, and reported using consistent assessment methods across schools or districts, as applicable.

In contrast to common assessments, educator-created assessments often purpose to measure a smaller group of students' learning, sometimes limited to one particular grade level or an individual class. Designed by either one educator or collaboratively among a team of colleagues, such assessments serve to determine how comprehensively learners have grasped knowledge of skills within more narrow contexts. These assessment types may involve a variety of formats, including fill in the blank, multiple choice, matching, essay, and other question types.

Performance assessments, otherwise known as "authentic assessments," involve learner-created products such as writing pieces, hands-on experiments, speeches, presentations, and/or portfolios. The successful completion of these assessments necessitates critical thinking and problem-solving endeavors. Furthermore, they entail varied applications of learning to real-world contexts or experiences; consequently, authentic assessment outcomes naturally involve a great extent of diversity. Rubrics or scoring guides help educators and students to begin with the end in mind throughout the discussion, creation, review, and evaluation process for each authentic artifact of learning.

In nearly any educational setting, authentic assessments offer educators and learners more purposeful evaluations of knowledge and skills acquired; they also provide educators with a means of gauging strengths and weaknesses in relation to the delivery of instruction and the student learning that results. Such assessment types integrate evaluations of content knowledge with experiences that involve the application of meaningful skills utilized in real-life situations. Resultantly, they play a vital role in measuring (and promoting) students' grasp of key knowledge and skills within today's digital age.

FORWARD-THINKING ASSESSMENT DESIGN

Educational experiences of today do not (and cannot) resemble educational experiences of the past. In the present digital world, professional settings consistently change as new technological developments come to be, calling for a steady reskilling of workers. Such technological advancements have necessitated a vaster reskilling across various professional contexts than the world has ever before seen. The concept of future-focused assessment design is overviewed in relation to technology integration in *Collegial Coaching: Mentoring for Knowledge and Skills That Transfer to Real-World Applications* (Alaniz, 2021); however, this paradigm ultimately applies to any assessment endeavor:

> Today's educators must remain mindful of the fact that they are preparing learners for jobs that might not even exist at this point. According to a report published by Dell Technologies and the Institute for the Future (2018), 85 percent of the jobs that will exist in 2030 have not even been invented yet. Although teachers in today's classrooms might not be able to predict what types of professions their students will pursue in the future, they can help them develop the skills they will need to successfully encounter any job opportunity—even those that have not yet been invented! Teachers in today's world are charged with the task of helping students dive into the DEEP end of learning experiences, supporting them as they **discover, engage, experiment,** and **produce**. (p. 93)

Rather than relying solely upon traditional assessment methods such as quizzes and exams, educators should design assessment measures by first reflecting upon what future-focused knowledge and skills they ultimately want students to acquire. Within the previously mentioned white paper highlighting novel instructional strategies for deep learning endeavors, Fullan and Scott (2014, pp. 6–7) presented the idea of "Six C's" of learning within today's digital age, offering these descriptions:

- Character: "Qualities of the individual essential for being personally effective in a complex world, including grit, tenacity, perseverance, resilience, reliability, and honesty"
- Citizenship: "Thinking like global citizens, considering global issues based on a deep understanding of diverse values with

genuine interest in engaging with others to solve complex problems that impact human and environmental sustainability"
- Collaboration: "The capacity to work interdependently and synergistically in teams with strong interpersonal and team-related skills including effective management of team dynamics, making substantive decisions together, and learning from and contributing to the learning of others"
- Communication: "Mastery of three fluencies: digital, writing, and speaking tailored for a range of audiences"
- Creativity: "Having an 'entrepreneurial eye' for economic and social opportunities, asking the right questions to generate novel ideas, and demonstrating leadership to pursue those ideas into practice"
- Critical Thinking: "Critically evaluating information and arguments, seeing patterns and connections, construction meaningful knowledge and applying it in the real world"

In many academic, professional, and personal contexts within today's digital age, individuals face the temptation to pursue the "latest and greatest" technological tools and resources—sometimes, at nearly any cost. This preoccupation may easily distract educators and educational leaders from focusing on truly impactful, future-focused learning. In reality, no matter how cutting-edge a device may seem, that device will eventually represent an outdated (and oftentimes outrageously expensive) technology.

Case in point: Thinking back to October 1, 1982, a groundbreaking new device was released by Sony called the compact disc (CD) player. Many individuals clamored to get their hands on this device, typically paying upward of $1,000 or more to procure one (the equivalent of $3,028.97 in 2022). By 1985, sales were rapidly accelerating. For many years, CD players represented the "latest and greatest" in commercially available devices for listening to pre-recorded digital audio. In 2003, the sales of CDs started to decline, correlating with the release of the iPod in 2001. Today, CDs and CD players are sold in some antique stores, alongside cassettes and the cassette players that were considered "cutting-edge" before the advent of DVDs.

Those clamoring to purchase CDs might never have imagined that services such as Spotify would eventually allow them to listen to every song imaginable at the touch of a button or the tap of a screen, without the purchase or use of a specialized listening device or compact disc. While the "latest and greatest" is often accompanied by mass appeal and excitement, something "bigger and better" will always eventually come along, in educational settings and beyond. What is most important is not the digital tools that are used. Far more significantly, solid content and instructional strategies should drive technology integration—and all classroom activities, rather than vice versa.

As described in *Collegial Coaching: Mentoring for Knowledge and Skills That Transfer to Real-World Applications* (Alaniz, 2021),

> Rather than focusing on using an interactive screen and having a device in every hand, teachers should be encouraged to provide opportunities for students to collaborate with classmates in solving real-world problems. Furthermore, they should facilitate experiences in which students create innovative products to share beyond the walls of their classroom. . . . Impactful teaching in today's world focuses on making learning experiences authentic or more meaningful for students. When students are given opportunities to envision how they might use targeted knowledge and skills within a variety of future contexts, they will more naturally remain engaged and motivated throughout the learning process, ultimately make learning more memorable! (p. 94)

A TIME FOR EVERY ASSESSMENT FORMAT

Just as educators plan lessons to address a wide array of learning goals, assessment formats may be designed to evaluate a variety of distinct facets throughout students' learning processes. For instance, assessments may be directed toward evaluating students' existing content knowledge or skills, thereby confirming their level of preparation for a forthcoming unit or lesson (**pre-assessments**).

On the other hand, some assessments measure students' learning amid an instructional cycle, thus allowing educators to adjust upcoming instructional delivery in response to students' progress (**formative assessments**). Alternatively, assessments may determine the extent of learning because of, or at the conclusion of, an instructional cycle (**summative assessments**).

Prior to the start of new instructional cycles, pre-assessments may be delivered to assess learners' existing knowledge. Such pre-assessments support educators in deciphering the extent of knowledge and skills their students possess before introducing novel concepts. Pre-assessments represent the "K" component of the timeless, widely utilized advance organizer known as a KWL chart. These charts underscore what learners presently **know**, what they **want** to eventually know, and, in due course, what they will **learn** throughout a unit or lesson to come. Pre-assessments provide instructional direction, possibly saving time as educators identify already-mastered concepts to eliminate.

In addition to pre-assessments, formative assessments also accomplish important goals within instructional cycles. As described by Wilson, Alaniz, and Sikora (2016) in *Digital Media in Today's Classrooms: The Potential for Meaningful Teaching, Learning, and Assessment*,

> As an informal measure of students' emergent learning, these assessments provide teachers with insights needed to fine-tune teaching and learning as they are occurring. Additionally, they inform educators of any existing need for reteaching prior to the conclusion of the lesson and direct teachers in future instructional decision making. Ultimately, formal assessments serve as a trial run for students and a check for understanding in the midst of the learning process. Examples include questioning, discussion, graphic organizers, and exit slips, among countless other options. (p. 108)

Finally, summative assessments measure the learning that has taken place by an instructional cycle's conclusion. These assessments may evaluate a student's learning in comparison to a predetermined standard or benchmark. Summative assessments represent a more formal measure or learning than formative assessments. They typically showcase a student's success in learning key facets of a unit or lesson through a point valuation method. Often utilized examples include a final paper, a capstone project, or a formal presentation. Insights gathered as a result of summative assessments might be applied in a formative manner as educators or their students allow these insights to guide future instruction and learning endeavors.

PURPOSE-DRIVEN ASSESSMENT PRACTICES

The process of assessing authentic learning endeavors involves a different process than scoring a more traditional assessment type such as a quiz or exam. As they design authentic assessment endeavors and evaluate students' resultant artifacts of learning, educators must decide how successfully the final product evidences the desired knowledge and skills.

In the words of Wilson, Alaniz, and Sikora (2016),

> Skillfully designed criteria-based rubrics enable students to apprehend specifically how their work will be evaluated, even before they begin the project. This way, students—and not just their teachers—receive the opportunity to "begin with the end in mind," focusing more specifically and purposefully on meeting predetermined criteria for excellence, rather than blindly and haphazardly piecing together their project. Rubrics may support teachers in alleviating "surprise" elements of grading, as students gain insights regarding how the grading process will unfold. With the use of rubrics, issues may arise when students—especially those who are operating at higher levels—begin to "aim low," just barely meeting the requirements outlined in the rubric rather than striving for excellence. These situations may be avoided by adding features to the rubric to encourage students to reach their fullest potential through unconventional methods. "Creativity points" or points for "going above and beyond" in unique ways might encourage additional innovation from learners. (p. 119)

Rubrics may also serve as an excellent tool for facilitating peer review prior to an assignment's final due date. This approach encourages collaboration and allows for reciprocal learning experiences as students practice the art of effectively receiving and implementing feedback, as well as asking meaningful questions and offering constructive feedback. The process of reviewing one another's artifacts of learning through the lens of a rubric allows the reviewer and the reviewee to examine submissions more critically, possibly even with a heightened sense of purpose and focus.

Another benefit of using rubrics concerns their facilitation of increased communication and transparency as graded assessments are reviewed. Although students may enjoy surprises when it comes to birthdays and gifts, most do not appreciate surprises where grading is concerned. Effectively designed rubrics offer valuable insights for educators and their students as they discuss learning outcomes and steps necessary to achieve those outcomes through future assessment endeavors.

Representative Rubrics to Guide the Authentic Assessment Journey

The final section of this chapter provides an array of rubric design tools and resources, as well as sample rubrics that may be utilized to evaluate authentic assessment endeavors within classroom contexts. Any rubrics incorporated within an educational setting should be customized to specifically address instructional purposes and student learning outcomes aligned with each discipline, developmental level, unit, lesson, and group of individual leaners. Additionally, learners should be trained in exploring, understanding, and applying rubrics so that they are able to gain the most benefit from each assignment.

The rubrics in Tables 4.1 and 4.2 have been adapted from rubrics presented in *Digital Media in Today's Classrooms: The Potential for Meaningful Teaching, Learning, and Assessment* (Wilson, Alaniz, & Sikora, 2016).

Through the process of evaluating collaborative endeavors incorporating various student responsibilities and end products, educators may implement rubrics divided either by task, assignment, or both. In the event that the project requires learners to collaborate through each element, a rubric assessing participation or collaboration might be more appropriately applied. Rubrics such as the following may provide insights regarding each student's contribution to achieving the overarching goals and final outcomes surrounding the project.

A number of ready-made rubrics featured on many educational websites effectively address a vast array of student learning outcomes. Among these resources, Kathy Schrock's website offers many well-designed rubrics to address a variety of authentic assessment endeavors. Schrock's rubric web page includes various categories for assessing numerous artifacts of learning. These resources can be accessed via the following address: http://www.schrockguide.net/assessment-and-rubrics.html.

Table 4.1. Sample Digital Media Rubric for Assessment of a Project Created by an Individual Student.

Project Title: "Life Cycles in Nature"
Digital Tool Used: iMovie, Book Creator, or Other Digital Storytelling Tool

Criteria Topic	"Excellent" Criteria 10 points	"Acceptable" Criteria 7 points	"Poor" Criteria 4 Points
Pictures	Pictures are clear and give excellent added meaning to the life cycle process illustrated.	Pictures are mostly clear and give some added meaning to the life cycle process illustrated.	Some pictures are not clear and distract the viewer from learning the life cycle process.
Narration	Narrator does an **excellent** job describing at least three different life cycles.	Narrator does an **acceptable** job describing at least three different life cycles (or an excellent job describing just two examples).	Narrator does not illustrate the different stages of life cycles.
Music	Music effectively correlates with the content of the project and enhances the quality of the presentation.	Music seems an acceptable choice considering the content of the presentation.	Music does not seem to fit the content of the presentation.
Video Segments	Video segments effectively correlate with the content of the project and enhance the quality of the presentation.	Video segments seem an acceptable choice considering the content of the presentation.	Video segments do not seem to fit the content of the presentation.
Text	Text effectively correlates with the content of the project and enhances the quality of the presentation.	Text seems an acceptable choice considering the content of the presentation.	Text does not seem to fit the content of the presentation.

Font and Style	Font and style effectively correlate with the content of the project and enhance the quality of the presentation.	Font and style seem an acceptable choice considering the content of the presentation.	Font and style do not seem to fit the content of the presentation.
Creativity	Highly creative methods of describing the different types of life cycles are evident throughout the presentation.	Some creative methods are evident throughout the presentation.	Creative methods are not evident throughout the presentation. The individual did not incorporate creativity beyond what was expected.
Citations and References	The presentation includes citations and references for all resources used.	The presentation includes citations and references for most resources used.	The presentation includes few to no citations and references for resources used.

Figure 4.1. Kathy Schrock's Guide to Everything: Assessment and Rubrics

For educators seeking to design rubrics of their own, many websites exist specifically to support them in achieving this goal. Rubistar (http://rubistar.4teachers.org) is a useful tool for educators wanting to prepare their own rubrics without devoting the time to create them completely from scratch. A number of templates on this site enable educators to input precreated criteria, in addition to editing on the basis of unique SLOs addressed by specific assessment pieces.

Table 4.2.

Group Member Completing the Form: Sample Group Member 4
Group Participation Rubric
Group Member 1: _____

Criteria Topic	"Excellent" Criteria 10 points	"Acceptable" Criteria 7 points	"Poor" Criteria 4 points
Completed daily assignments on time. (Contributions)	Group member 1 always completed homework and assignments on time.	Group member 1 usually completed homework and assignments on time.	Group member 1 was often late on completing assigned work.
Worked well with others. (Attitude)	Group member 1 always worked well with the group.	Group member 1 usually worked well with the group.	Group member 1 didn't work well with the group.
Helped others on their assignments. (Teamwork)	Group member 1 helped me with my assignment.	Group member 1 didn't help me but didn't distract me on my assignment.	Group member 1 didn't help me and distracted me while working on my group assignment.
Stayed on task during class. (Effectiveness)	Group member 1 always did what the teacher expected in class.	Group member 1 usually did what the teacher expected in class.	Group member 1 caused distractions in class.

Group Member Completing the Form: Sample Group Member 4
Group Participation Rubric
Group Member 2: _____

Criteria Topic	"Excellent" Criteria 10 points	"Acceptable" Criteria 7 points	"Poor" Criteria 4 points
Completed daily assignments on time. (Contributions)	Group member 2 always completed homework and assignments on time.	Group member 2 usually completed homework and assignments on time.	Group member 2 was often late on completing assigned work.
Worked well with others. (Attitude)	Group member 2 always worked well with the group.	Group member 2 usually worked well with the group.	Group member 2 didn't work well with the group.
Helped others on their assignments. (Teamwork)	Group member 2 helped me with my assignment.	Group member 2 didn't help me but didn't distract me on my assignment.	Group member 2 didn't help me and distracted me while working on my group assignment.
Stayed on task during class. (Effectiveness)	Group member 2 always did what the teacher expected in class.	Group member 2 usually did what the teacher expected in class.	Group member 2 caused distractions in class.

Group Member Completing the Form: Sample Group Member 4
Group Participation Rubric
Group Member 3: _____

Criteria Topic	"Excellent" Criteria 10 points	"Acceptable" Criteria 7 points	"Poor" Criteria 4 points
Completed daily assignments on time. (Contributions)	Group member 3 always completed homework and assignments on time.	Group member 3 usually completed homework and assignments on time.	Group member 3 was often late on completing assigned work.
Worked well with others. (Attitude)	Group member 3 always worked well with the group.	Group member 3 usually worked well with the group.	Group member 3 didn't work well with the group.
Helped others on their assignments. (Teamwork)	Group member 3 helped me with my assignment.	Group member 3 didn't help me but didn't distract me on my assignment.	Group member 3 didn't help me and distracted me while working on my group assignment.
Stayed on task during class. (Effectiveness)	Group member 3 always did what the teacher expected in class.	Group member 3 usually did what the teacher expected in class.	Group member 3 caused distractions in class.

Figure 4.2. Rubistarhatt

TeAchnology (http://www.teach-nology.com/web_tools/rubrics/) also contains tools to develop customizable rubrics; additionally, the site provides educators access to a number of ready-made rubrics. Furthermore, TeAchnology includes resources to support students through engaging in authentic assessment endeavors, specifically involving digital tools and resources. It also provides free tutorials focusing on the design of digital products.

Figure 4.3. TeAchnology

Additionally, the University of Texas at Austin's Faculty Innovation Center offers a helpful guide (https://ctl.utexas.edu/sites/default/files/build-rubric.pdf) to answer the following questions:

- What is a rubric?
- What does a rubric look like?
- Where do I start the process of creating a rubric?
- How can I design a rubric?
- What can I consider as I review a rubric?
- Where can I learn more?

Exploring Assessments, Assessments, and More Assessments 49

Figure 4.4. The University of Texas at Austin Faculty Innovation Center Rubric Guide

ESSENTIAL IDEAS TO REMEMBER

Countless strategies exist for differentiating between assessment types and determining which type to utilize at various points in each instructional cycle. From formative to summative, from teacher-centered to student-centered (and every assessment type in between), the most effective educators intentionally seek to design applicable, meaningful assessments, no matter the assessment type utilized. They purposefully create future-focused authentic assessment endeavors that apply to real life and address skills needed for the days and years to come.

Additionally, they empower students to begin with the end in mind by crafting rubrics that address key student learning outcomes. By implementing a meaningful method for evaluating assessment pieces—whether formative or summative—educators effectively pave the way for students to achieve set SLOs. Clear-cut expectations help eliminate grading surprises and ultimately encourage a higher caliber of student work. As a result, educators support their learners in progressing steadily toward their triumphal crossing of the finish line of academic success, one step at a time.

REFERENCES

Abbott, S. (Ed.). (2015, November 10). Hidden curriculum, in *The glossary of education reform*. http://edglossary.org/hidden-curriculum

Alaniz, K. (2021). *Collegial coaching: Mentoring for knowledge and skills that transfer to real-world applications*. Lanham, MD: Rowman & Littlefield Education.

Fullan, M., & Scott, G. (2014). *New pedagogies for deep learning whitepaper: Education PLUS.* Seattle, WA: Collaborative Impact SPC.

Institute for the Future (IFTF), for Dell Technologies. (2018). *Realizing 2030: A divided vision of the future: Global business leaders forecast the next era of human-machine partnerships and how they intend to prepare* [summary]. https://www.delltechnologies.com/content/dam/delltechnologies/assets/perspectives/2030/pdf/Realizing-2030-A-Divided-Vision-of-the-Future-Summary.pdf

Willis, J. (2008). *Teaching the brain to read: Strategies for improving fluency, vocabulary, and comprehension.* Alexandria, VA: Association for Supervision and Curriculum Development.

Wilson, D., Alaniz, K., & Sikora, J. (2016). *Digital media in today's classrooms: The potential for meaningful teaching, learning, and assessment.* Lanham, MD: Rowman & Littlefield Education.

Chapter 5

Making It All Add Up

How Does the Formula for Authentic Learning Apply?

"Education is what remains after one has forgotten everything he learned in school."

—Albert Einstein

As educators plan and implement authentic learning endeavors, students benefit from memorable and meaningful learning experiences that transfer to the world beyond the walls of the classroom. The most effective educators understand that they inspire intrinsic motivation to learn when learning is applicable to real life outside of educational contexts. Authentic learning experiences hold the potential to completely transform learning endeavors as students transition from passive consumers of information to active cocreators of meaningful learning opportunities. As remarked by George Couros, a teaching and leadership consultant and speaker, "Learning is creation, not consumption. Knowledge is not something a learner absorbs, but something a learner creates."

A formula for authentic learning is presented within the book *Collegial Coaching: Mentoring for Knowledge and Skills That Transfer to Real-World Applications* (Alaniz, 2021); educators facilitate such learning endeavors through intentional instructional strategies founded in applicability:

> They do this by offering [students] real-world problems to solve, giving them opportunities to present solutions to various audiences, and designing assessment endeavors that apply to the everyday lives of learners. This method is summed up in an innovative formula for meaningful learning: authentic issues + authentic audiences + authentic assessment = authentic learning experiences. (p. 92)

This formula finds its basis in several key principles overviewed in previous chapters, including the tenants of beginning with the end in mind and starting with WHY. Benjamin Disraeli, twice prime minister of the United Kingdom, famously remarked, "The secret of success is constancy to purpose." Without purpose in planning and executing, educators will almost certainly find themselves unable to inspire purpose and passion for learning within their students.

Legendary American football coach Vince Lombardi echoed this sentiment in his statement regarding the importance of purpose: "Success demands singleness of purpose." As educators introduce student learning outcomes and corresponding assessment endeavors to learners, the WHY must remain at the forefront. This inspires intrinsic motivation for learning, perseverance through academic challenges, and success in achieving student learning outcomes. The power of intrinsic motivation to impact student learning cannot be overstated. As remarked by Leonardo da Vinci, "Just as eating contrary to the inclination is injurious to the health, so study without desire spoils the memory, and it retains nothing that it takes in."

Purpose is accomplished through aligning learning endeavors with real life, as students discern meaningful ways in which their experiences in the classroom translate to their life beyond the walls of the classroom. As they recognize ties between the knowledge and skills inherent in learning outcomes and their current or future personal or professional experiences, they naturally become more invested in academic pursuits. As discussed in chapter 4, while today's educators may not know what future professional paths students will eventually take, they do have the opportunity to support them in gaining skills that will be necessary in any future professional context.

The aforementioned white paper by Fullan and Scott (2014, pp. 6–7) highlights the following novel instructional strategies for future-focused learning:

- Character: "Qualities of the individual essential for being personally effective in a complex world, including grit, tenacity, perseverance, resilience, reliability, and honesty"
- Citizenship: "Thinking like global citizens, considering global issues based on a deep understanding of diverse values with genuine interest in engaging with others to solve complex problems that impact human and environmental sustainability"
- Collaboration: "The capacity to work interdependently and synergistically in teams with strong interpersonal and team-related skills including effective management of team dynamics, making substantive decisions together, and learning from and contributing to the learning of others"
- Communication: "Mastery of three fluencies: digital, writing, and speaking tailored for a range of audiences"
- Creativity: "Having an 'entrepreneurial eye' for economic and social opportunities, asking the right questions to generate novel ideas, and demonstrating leadership to pursue those ideas into practice"
- Critical Thinking: "Critically evaluating information and arguments, seeing patterns and connections, construction meaningful knowledge and applying it in the real world"

The importance of providing learners with applicable opportunities to develop these skills becomes particularly apparent when considering the ways in which professional settings have evolved over time—and will continue to evolve. If asked to name five lucrative occupations in today's professional contexts that did not exist 20 years ago, jobs such as the following might come to mind:

- Social media manager
- Cryptocurrency expert
- Digital marketing specialist
- Search engine optimization (SEO) specialist
- App developer
- Career coach
- Cloud computing specialist
- College admissions consultant
- Online shop (Etsy, Poshmark, etc.) owner
- Social media influencer

Although the thought of earning a lucrative salary through several of the above-listed professional avenues may seem a bit difficult to fathom, this list includes a variety of occupations through which many individuals support themselves and their families, with income to spare. What do these professional endeavors have in common? Beyond the fact that they are comparatively recent, burgeoning occupational opportunities, those who are successful in these professions typically also demonstrate exceptional skill in many, if not most, of the "Six C's" of learning in the digital age.

Case in point: For a social media influencer, creativity is a must; they create content and introduce chosen products through innovative strategies. Social media influencers must also be able to communicate in ways that effectively appeal to their intended audience. Additionally, they must be able to collaborate with select corporate partners in order to successfully showcase highlighted products. In doing so, they must think critically, insightfully addressing issues while serving as a liaison between their sponsors and their audiences. Finally, those influencers who demonstrate character and citizenship as they interact with sponsors and the public will likely be far more successful in the long run than those who engage in deceptive or irresponsible practices.

Twenty or more years ago, educators might not have imagined that their classes contained individuals who would grow up to be influencers, digital marketing specialists, and app developers. Today's educators cannot possibly predict the careers their students will pursue in 10 years, let alone 20. Yet, by equipping them with the "Six C's" of learning in the digital age, they will more effectively prepare them to face an ever-changing world with confidence, resourcefulness, impact, and success.

In their book *Generation Z Unfiltered: Facing Nine Hidden Challenges of the Most Anxious Population*, Elmore and McPeak (2019) reveal that this generation is more interested in leading than the previous three generations. Educators invested in cultivating the Six C's and authentic assessment experiences will prepare younger generations to effectively lead. These skills flourish through authentic learning experiences. The following formula for authentic learning is covered in greater depth throughout the remainder of this chapter: authentic issues + authentic audiences + authentic assessment = authentic learning experiences (Alaniz, 2021).

ADDRESSING AUTHENTIC ISSUES

In order to lead productive lives, adults necessarily engage in decision-making processes and problem-solving experiences innumerable times over the course of each day. In doing so, they discover solutions to various real-life issues. However, many of today's learners struggle to effectively problem-solve. This may be because many are seldom exposed to substantial opportunities to tackle meaningful issues and to solve significant problems. Students spend the majority of their waking hours in classroom settings; their time devoted to schooling occupies a sizable percentage of highly pivotal years. For this reason, it is tremendously important that learners confront and engage in problem-solving opportunities during their years spent in school.

Aungst (2015), whose areas of expertise include mathematics curricular development, digital literacy, and gifted education, is the author of *Five Principles of the Modern Mathematics Classroom*. Aungst presents five steps to fostering a problem-solving culture within educational settings: conjecture, communication, collaboration, chaos, and celebration. An edWeb (2014) webinar featuring Aungst highlights insights regarding problem-solving experiences that extend beyond mathematics curricular content. Aungst contends that rather than needing more people who excel at math in particular, the world needs more people skilled at solving problems—individuals who are innovators.

Rather than viewing challenging problems as impossible to solve, innovators seek out problems and attempt to solve them before anyone else recognizes that the problem even existed in the first place. Instead of endeavoring to offer solutions every time a problem presents itself, insightful educators avoid presenting an answer at the conclusion of each unit or lesson. As an alternative, they ask students to describe what they believe to be a potential answer, how they discovered a solution, and whether other solutions exist. Assessment experiences should include opportunities to seek out and uncover problems to solve.

Along the lines of Aungst's (2015) five principles, a helpful digital resource to facilitate opportunities for the "conjecture" component of this process is Data.gov (https://data.gov/). As students explore this site and come across unfamiliar data, they might be asked to form an opinion or conclusion on the basis of incomplete information.

Figure 5.1. Data.gov

Through the "communication" component of the five principles, students gain practice with explaining their thinking, in turn developing their knowledge. It is important that students develop the ability to expound upon possible solutions through their own words; in doing so, they build skills that can be incorporated in every area of life, no matter the professional pursuits they select. Tools to facilitate practice with communicating effectively include Piktochart (https://piktochart.com/) and Infogram (https://infogram.com/).

Figure 5.2. Piktochart

Figure 5.3. Infogram

The "collaboration" facet impacts innumerable areas of everyday life, as real-world problem-solving endeavors often involve collaboration. As they partner in problem-solving activities, students consider others' perspectives, taking part in reciprocal learning endeavors. A myriad of digital tools and resources can be applied to encourage problem-solving exercises, such as cloud-based Google products including Google Slides, Google Docs, and Google Sheets, in addition to online Microsoft Office 365 products such as PowerPoint, Word, and Excel.

The "chaos" element of problem-solving acknowledges that the nature of problem-solving endeavors is not often straightforward. Rather, problem-solving is typically somewhat messy. Students should be given opportunities to grapple with problems in purposeful ways, thus making learning experiences more applicable and meaningful.

Finally, the "celebration" component includes opportunities to emphasize students' development and successes, in addition to setbacks that will ultimately bring about new growth. Effective educators validate learners' efforts, not simply their correct answers. Students should be encouraged to persevere, even when their initial answers are incorrect. In her book titled *Grit: The Power of Passion and Perseverance*, Duckworth (2016) identified the importance of both passion and perseverance in meeting goals. Effective educators establish a culture in which they and their students learn and grow in the face of setbacks. In the words of notable leadership author and renowned speaker John Maxwell, "Fail early, fail often, but always fail forward."

Community gardens established by students offer an outstanding example of educationally based problem-solving endeavors. For example, in the Houston metropolitan area, Urban Harvest (https://www.urbanharvest.org/education/youth/school-partnerships/) encourages school communities to initiate and cultivate gardens, providing nutrition courses to discover healthy eating habits, ecosystems, and native habitats. This project bridges communities with local schools, giving students opportunities to collaborate with, communicate with, and serve alongside one another to create positive change within their communities. As they take part in service-based experiential learning, they naturally work toward solving real-world problems that will impact the communities in which they live for the better.

Figure 5.4. Urban Harvest

COMMUNICATING WITH AUTHENTIC AUDIENCES

Authentic learning opportunities provide students the chance to communicate their newfound knowledge and skills with others, encouraging them to prepare their best work prior to sharing with an audience. When students realize that their assignments will be viewed not only by their teacher, they often become even more motivated to produce artifacts of learning that showcase their new learning. In a progressively more connected world, digital tools and resources provide vast platforms and opportunities for learners to display their work beyond their classroom settings for real-world audiences to discover.

In alignment with the backward design framework overviewed in chapter 3, an initial step toward identifying an appropriate authentic audience involves reflecting upon the desired results and articulating applicable student learning outcomes. Next, educators should think through the format for the project. Maybe learners will collaborate to solve a problem within their community by applying concepts they have discovered in social studies. Perhaps they will explore an issue involving current events they have discussed in their history lessons. When student learning outcomes are pinpointed prior to the creation process, an intended audience will more easily come to light.

The importance of providing learners the opportunity to present to diverse audiences is described in *Collegial Coaching: Mentoring for Knowledge and Skills That Transfer to Real-World Applications* (Alaniz, 2021):

> Authentic audiences should vary from project to project, providing students with opportunities to apply developing skills in the presence of different groups of people. Teachers may begin by seeking familiar audience members, such as family, friends, or others who already have an interest in students' lives. Learners might also present their creations to others within the school setting, such as students in other classes or grade levels as well as administrators or instructional support specialists. It may also be helpful to seek the support of experts in the field. For example, students working on an impressionist painting project in art class might host a gallery walk and invite a local artist to tour the exhibit. (p. 97)

Making It All Add Up 59

Mathtrain.TV (http://mathtrain.tv/) provides an impactful example of how exposure to authentic audiences empowers learners to produce purposeful work. Students at Lincoln Middle School in Santa Monica, California, collaboratively create math screencasts shared through the site; these student-created tutorials are viewed by audiences around the world. As students create these popular videos, they utilize critical thinking to meaningfully communicate strategies for problem-solving.

Figure 5.5. Mathtrain.TV

At the time of publication, Mathtrain.TV has been accessed by more than 60,000 people in countries across the globe. What a testimony to the power of authentic audiences! It is easy to imagine the sense of purpose and empowerment students at Lincoln Middle School must feel knowing that the math tutorials they create impact thousands of individuals they may never even meet.

CREATING IMPACTFUL AUTHENTIC ASSESSMENTS

As described by Alaniz (2021),

> [Authentic assessments] provide a revealing glimpse of what learners actually know and what they can actually do, rather than simply showcasing how skillfully students can take quizzes or exams. Authentic assessments provide opportunities for learners to create novel end products, rather than simply requiring that they consume information for the purpose of regurgitating it while taking a quiz or exam. (p. 91)

In fact, within the Master of Science in Learning, Technology, and Design program at the authors' university, courses do not include any exams or quizzes. Instead, they include varied authentic assessment experiences that apply to students' current or future instructional design endeavors. Within each course, learners create artifacts of learning that provide evidence of their acquisition of student learning outcomes. As they begin with the end in mind, students design original digital tools and resources to incorporate within their professional contexts.

These aspiring instructional designers plan and implement assessment pieces with intentionality, intrinsically motivated by the knowledge that their own learners will benefit from their endeavors. Resultantly, finished products showcase excellence in instructional design, and students often express excitement to share their digital portfolios complete with a variety of artifacts of learning. In fact, students often add a portfolio link to the signature of their email or include a QR code in their résumé to direct others within professional networks to their impressive portfolio creations. Numerous students have been hired, received professional awards, or been offered promotions on the basis of their noteworthy digital portfolios.

The QR code below links to an exemplary portfolio created by a Master of Science in Learning, Technology, and Design graduate named Julie Blackwell (https://julieblackwell.weebly.com/portfolio.html).

Figure 5.6. Julie Blackwell's Professional Portfolio

ESSENTIAL IDEAS TO REMEMBER

Authentic learning endeavors indelibly impact students' experiences at school, as well as their lives beyond their schooling years. As educators develop academic endeavors that directly apply to the everyday world of learners, students gain knowledge and skills that transfer to new learning endeavors. The following encompasses an innovative formula for meaningful learning: authentic issues + authentic audiences + authentic assessment = authentic learning experiences.

Excellent educators inspire intrinsic motivation to learn by journeying with students through each step of new learning adventures as they introduce learners to real-world problems to solve, offer them opportunities to communicate solutions with various audiences, and create assessment experiences that apply in meaningful ways to learners' lives.

REFERENCES

Alaniz, K. (2021). *Collegial coaching: Mentoring for knowledge and skills that transfer to real-world applications.* Lanham, MD: Rowman & Littlefield Education.

Aungst, G. (2015). *Five principles of the modern mathematics classroom: Creating a culture of innovative thinking.* Thousand Oaks, CA: Corwin.

Duckworth, A. (2016). *Grit: The power of passion and perseverance* (Vol. 234). New York: Scribner.

edWeb (2014, August 20). Creating a culture of problem solving in your school or classroom. https://home.edweb.net/creating-culture-problem-solving-school-classroom/

Elmore, T., & McPeak, A. (2019). *Generation Z unfiltered: Facing nine hidden challenges of the most anxious population.* Atlanta, GA: Poet Gardener Publishing.

Fullan, M., & Scott, G. (2014). *New pedagogies for deep learning whitepaper: Education PLUS.* Seattle, WA: Collaborative Impact SPC.

Chapter 6

Embracing the Digital Age

How Do Technology Considerations Impact Assessment Strategies?

> *"Teachers need to integrate technology seamlessly into the curriculum instead of viewing it as an add-on, an afterthought, or an event."*
>
> —Heidi Hayes Jacobs

In a world in which digital innovation pervades all areas of society, the only constant is change. Various individuals respond to novel technological developments in any number of ways, ranging from overjoyed enthusiasm to total indifference to absolute resistance. Although innovators and change agents may not understand why some people struggle so greatly to accept new technological developments, author Calestous Juma seeks to empathize.

He believes that many valid reasons exist for the opposition to novel technologies. These reasons are overviewed within Juma's (2016) book titled *Innovation and Its Enemies: Why People Resist New Technologies*. Juma contends that as individuals consider the impact of digital innovation, their perception of the absence of the essence of humanity contributes to their skepticism. According to Juma, history records decades upon decades of humankind's resistance to technological advances.

Juma's work draws from 600 years of controversies surrounding new technologies, fluctuating from attacks regarding the coffee trade in the medieval Middle East and Europe to present-day debates surrounding the possible effects of innovations such as artificial intelligence, 3D printing, drones, and gene editing. Juma contends that humans are inclined to refuse novel technologies when they seem to substitute for, rather than enhance or strengthen, people's inherent humanity. Simply put, human beings desire to humanize technology.

While the natural tendency involves rejecting technologies that subtract from humanness, people typically embrace digital innovation that augments the natural desire for social inclusion, a sense of purpose, challenging endeavors, and the development of meaning. This is the case even when technological developments come at a significant expense, and even when learning to use them requires a substantial investment of time.

These principles hold true in educational environments as well as other segments of society; as discussed in the book *Collegial Coaching: Mentoring for Knowledge and Skills That Transfer to Real-World Applications* (Alaniz, 2021),

> In educational environments, the promise of digital integration is vast. It holds the potential to advance learning opportunities for students around the world. When executed efficaciously, educational technology often enhances the scope and impact of skillfully executed teaching (Lei & Zhao, 2007). It provides teachers with groundbreaking tools for reimagining the transfer of key concepts, thereby inspiring students to become cocreators of their own learning endeavors. The issue resides in the fact that technology incorporation fluctuates depending on the content area at hand and the developmental levels involved in the learning. (p. 42)

Digital innovation brings about many exciting promises within educational settings.

Yet, unless educators grasp the WHY for integrating technology, these promises hold little value. Like most human beings, educators must discern the purpose of digital incorporation before they can embrace its advantages. Unless they perceive the association between technology integration and a sense of purpose, the opportunity for challenging learning endeavors, and the development of new meaning, they will likely not be motivated to incorporate digital tools and resources within their instructional endeavors.

In the words of John Dewey, "If we teach today as we taught yesterday, we rob our children of tomorrow." In order for students to be prepared for the future, they must engage in innovative, future-focused learning endeavors today. Yet, this does not mean that educators should cram digital tools and resources into every lesson simply for the sake of ensuring that technology has been "integrated." In fact, student learning outcomes should drive technology integration and not vice versa.

When educators feel pressured to incorporate digital tools and resources without clear purpose and intentional planning, these technologies may offer more harm than benefit. School districts and families would be wise to question the WHY for a given technology rather than focusing on integration for the sake of integration.

THE TPACK FRAMEWORK

In reference to the necessity of purpose in instructional technology integration, the TPACK framework (Herring, Koehler, & Mishra, 2016) foundationally connects content and pedagogical aspects of teaching and learning, paralleling them with the incorporation of digital tools and resources. TPACK addresses the interrelationship between the following three primary forms of knowledge: content (CK), pedagogy (PK), and technology (TK).

Instead of focusing upon these three components independently, this framework emphasizes the variations of knowledge that exist in the intersections of the three knowledge types: pedagogical content knowledge (PCK), technological content knowledge (TCK), technological pedagogical knowledge (TPK), and technological pedagogical content knowledge (TPACK).

As stated by Alaniz (2021),

> Successful technology implementation requires effective pedagogical practices to convey essential content knowledge. . . . Individual students, unique teachers, differing developmental levels, shifting school settings, diverse demographics, and countless other factors guarantee that each circumstance will be unique. No one amalgamation of content, pedagogy, and technology will effectively serve students in every context. (p. 80)

The following list offers a summary of the diverse knowledge types constructed by Koehler (2012), one of the original designers of this classic educational framework:

- Content Knowledge (CK): "Teachers' knowledge about the subject matter to be learned or taught. The content to be covered in middle school science or history is different from the content to be covered in an undergraduate course on art appreciation or a graduate seminar on astrophysics. As Shulman (1986) noted, this knowledge would include knowledge of concepts, theories, ideas, organizational frameworks, knowledge of evidence and proof, as well as established practices and approaches toward developing such knowledge" (Koehler & Mishra, 2009).
- Pedagogical Knowledge (PK): "Teachers' deep knowledge about the processes and practices or methods of teaching and learning. They encompass, among other things, overall educational purposes, values, and aims. This generic form of knowledge applies to understanding how students learn, general classroom management skills, lesson planning, and student assessment" (Koehler & Mishra, 2009).
- Technology Knowledge (TK): "Knowledge about integrating technological tools and resources. This encompasses a broad enough understanding of technology that it can be applied in professional settings as well as in day-to-day life. This also entails recognition of when digital tools and resources can support or inhibit accomplishing set goals, as well as continued adaptation to as technological innovations occur" (Koehler & Mishra, 2009).
- Pedagogical Content Knowledge (PCK): "Consistent with and similar to Shulman's idea of knowledge of pedagogy that is applicable to the teaching of specific content. Central to Shulman's conceptualization of PCK is the notion of the transformation of the subject matter for teaching. Specifically, according to Shulman (1986), this transformation occurs as the teacher interprets the subject matter, finds multiple ways to represent it, and adapts and tailors the instructional materials to alternative conceptions and students' prior knowledge. PCK covers the core business of teaching, learning, curriculum, assessment, and reporting, such as the

conditions that promote learning and the links among curriculum, assessment, and pedagogy" (Koehler & Mishra, 2009).
- Technological Content Knowledge (TCK): "An understanding of the manner in which technology and content influence and constrain one another. Teachers need to master more than the subject matter they teach; they must also have a deep understanding of the manner in which the subject matter (or the kinds of representations that can be constructed) can be changed by the application of particular technologies. Teachers need to understand which specific technologies are best suited for addressing subject-matter learning in their domains and how the content dictates or perhaps even changes the technology—or vice versa" (Koehler & Mishra, 2009).
- Technological Pedagogical Knowledge (TPK): "An understanding of how teaching and learning can change when particular technologies are used in particular ways. This includes knowing the pedagogical affordances and constraints of a range of technological tools as they relate to disciplinarily and developmentally appropriate pedagogical designs and strategies" (Koehler & Mishra, 2009).
- Technological Pedagogical Content Knowledge (TPACK): "Underlying truly meaningful and deeply skilled teaching with technology, TPACK is different from knowledge of all three concepts individually. Instead, TPACK is the basis of effective teaching with technology, requiring an understanding of the representation of concepts using technologies; pedagogical techniques that use technologies in constructive ways to teach content; knowledge of what makes concepts difficult or easy to learn and how technology can help redress some of the problems that students face; knowledge of students' prior knowledge and theories of epistemology; and knowledge of how technologies can be used to build on existing knowledge to develop new epistemologies or strengthen old ones" (Koehler & Mishra, 2009).

As digital tools and resources are incorporated with purpose in alignment with content knowledge and sound instructional strategies (as directed by the TPACK framework), opportunities for meaningful technology integration abound.

> Rather than merely sprinkling technology into instructional practices because it seems new or exciting, teachers must first develop a clear

understanding of the goals and objectives upon which units and lessons will be built. . . . For example, technology may be employed by educators to augment instruction through video resources and presentations that deliver content through multiple modalities to support both auditory and visual learners. Technology provides teachers with strategies to demonstrate content through diverse media formats, including text, audio content, videos, hands-on modeling, and countless other applications. (Alaniz, 2021, p. 85)

ASSESSING WITH PURPOSE

Assessment plays a key role in evaluating the effectiveness of educational technologies; prior to commencing the assessment process, educators should first decipher the purpose of the digital tool and/or resource. This process heavily depends on whether the educational technologies to be utilized are educator-created or student-created.

The effectiveness of educator-created digital tools and resources depends upon how successfully such instructional endeavors support content area goals. This may be accomplished through measuring students' growth resulting from the unit or lesson in which the digital tools and/or resources were incorporated. KWL charts and other similar tools serve to informally evaluate learning, whereas individual pre- and post-content assessments measure learning in a more formal way.

As described by Wilson, Alaniz, and Sikora (2016) in *Digital Media in Today's Classrooms: The Potential for Meaningful Teaching, Learning, and Assessment*,

> The process of assessing student-created digital media pieces entails a somewhat different perspective and premise. Teachers must determine not only whether the process of multimedia creation supports students in learning, but they must also ascertain how effectively the end product demonstrates acquired knowledge and skills. Skillfully designed criteria-based rubrics enable students to comprehend specifically how their work will be evaluated, even before they begin the project. This way, students—and not just their teachers—receive the opportunity to "begin with the end in mind," focusing more specifically and purposefully on meeting predetermined criteria for excellence, rather than blindly and haphazardly piecing together their projects. (p. 119)

Chapter 4 more fully describes strategies for effective rubric creation.

Assessing Both Substance and Structure

As students create artifacts of learning through digital formats, in addition to assessing content, educators and learners should also evaluate such products in terms of their structure. Considering the potential to convey insights through subtexts, images, music, and video, digital projects greatly rely upon design as a means of successfully conveying key aspects of content.

In the words of Wilson, Alaniz, and Sikora (2016),

> Unquestionably, issues arise when form contradicts content, potentially leading to audience confusion or distraction from the main message. For instance, if teachers expect students to create a video summarizing the content of a book but give no criteria for evaluating the grammatical and mechanical aspects of the text included within the video, learners may more likely ignore these important aspects of multimedia creation. Ultimately, poorly written text might distract from an otherwise well-designed video, thus causing viewers to overlook key content. (pp. 120–21)

Substance and style operate collaboratively, and both should be evaluated when assessment methods involve digital products. Key content considerations include the following (Wilson, Alaniz, & Sikora, 2016, p. 121):

- Content accuracy: Are the facts presented verifiable? Were they taken from valid and reliable sources?
- Content clarity: Does the final product convey a central theme or themes? Do the individual pieces serve to enhance one cohesive whole?
- Content creativity: Did the designer add certain unique elements to demonstrate his or her ability to innovate? What aspects of this project differentiate it from the others submitted?
- Content purposes: Do content and form align, or does form distract from the key messages of the content?
- Copyright considerations: Did the student adequately and accurately cite resources used throughout the presentation, including

text, image, music, and video clips? Is it apparent that the student sought to abide by fair use considerations, being careful to avoid too extensively using any one audio or video segment?

Undoubtedly, content is king when digital tools and resources support academic pursuits. Even still, poor form may reduce the impact of even the most poignant messages. Therefore, educators and their students must not neglect the significance of aesthetic value and excellent craftsmanship when creating digital artifacts of learning.

Among various indicators of aesthetic quality, the following list includes key points of focus for learners when designing digital tools and resources (Wilson, Alaniz, & Sikora, 2016, pp. 121–22):

- Font consistency: Do the style and size of the font increase readability and align with the theme of the project, or do they detract from the central message?
- Template consistency: How well do the chosen templates align with the key ideas conveyed through the multimedia piece? Do they support a central theme or seem disjointed?
- Animation or transitional consistency: Do animations and transitions add interest to the project and enhance audience engagement, or might they potentially befuddle and/or distract viewers?
- Color and style consistency: How effectively do other visual elements, such as color palettes and the style of the finished product, support the chief ideas expressed? Do they serve to draw attention to significant themes, or do they seem out of place?
- Image choices: Does the presentation contain high-quality images that support the audience in visualizing a central message, or do the images seem fuzzy and/or out of place in consideration of the prevailing theme?

While aesthetic effectiveness enhances content delivery, presentation quality also heavily impacts audience members' perceptions of and reactions to messages conveyed. Although students should be given consistent, meaningful opportunities to practice live presentation skills, experiences that develop video presentation skills should also be incorporated in learning endeavors. Especially within a world in which video-based content creation is increasingly more utilized in professional spheres, learners who have perfected the art of video creation will be even better prepared for future occupational experiences.

Assessment considerations surrounding video-based presentations vary greatly from those involving live presentations. The following list addresses a number of vital considerations for evaluating video-based presentations (Wilson, Alaniz, & Sikora, 2016, p. 123):

- Technical quality: Does the video contain clear, applicable images organized in a logical format? Are the exposure levels suitable, and was the camera held steady throughout shooting?
- Audio quality: Are the sound levels appropriate throughout the video? Does the narration and music blend well, or is the volume of one element disproportionate?
- Engaging quality: Do the text, image, narration, music, and video elements work cohesively to capture audience interest? Does the video contain dynamic developmental aspects that maintain viewers' curiosity and attentiveness?
- Cinematic quality: Does the video contain a transportive quality serving as a vehicle to transfer viewers' minds to another place and time? Is there an element of journalistic style conveying accuracy, brevity, and candor? How do motion, images, lighting, and color intermingle to add visual appeal of the piece? In what ways do sound and musical elements enhance the emotions inspired by the video? How is editing utilized to inspire intellectual curiosity and a sense of wonder?

ENSURING THAT INNOVATION AND EDUCATION GO HAND IN HAND

The task of identifying applicable digital tools and resources for learning once involved a more labor-intensive, time-consuming journey. This is no longer the case in a culture of bring-your-own-device (BYOD) academic programs, omnipresent Wi-Fi, and freely available digital tools and resources for educators and learners alike. With an abundance of tools and resources at their disposal, educators and their students no longer face a lack of innovative technologies; yet, they may lack the knowledge and skills needed to incorporate them responsibly within learning endeavors—and in life.

As with most considerations surrounding educational transformation, clear-cut answers may not exist, and numerous decisions must be made. For educators responsible for the well-being and effective development of future generations, student safety represents the most critical of these considerations.

As remarked by Wilson, Alaniz, and Sikora (2016),

> Just as administrators, faculty, and staff members are responsible for the physical safety of the students under their care at school each day, they are also liable for the online safety of these students. By the same token, as teachers instinctively guide their students in becoming responsible citizens of the communities in which they live, they must also learn to lead today's younger generations in developing the mindsets and habits of responsible digital and global citizens. . . . While many forward-thinking teachers delight in the prospect of introducing innovative, engaging digital tools to their students, fewer numbers consider the imperative of doing so in correlation with instruction in digital citizenship. Yet, these two endeavors must go hand in hand. (p. 34)

Through the help of administrators, digital learning specialists, information technology directors, and curriculum coordinators, academic communities can actively support educators and parents in becoming increasingly informed and involved in student privacy and data retention issues. Additionally, as these stakeholders collaborate to enhance digital safety awareness, they support students in becoming advocates for their own safety and the protection of their online privacy throughout their academic careers and into their future professional lives.

Fortunately, many highly effective, comprehensive resources exist for empowering stakeholders in the process of developing online safety measures and enhancing students' knowledge and skills in this area. For instance, Common Sense Media (https://www.commonsensemedia.org/) frequently publishes resources pertaining to students' online privacy and protection, thereby supporting expanded knowledge regarding the rights and responsibilities of students as digital consumers and content creators.

Figure 6.1. Common Sense Media

Coping with COPPA

The Children's Online Privacy and Protection Act (COPPA), regulated by the Federal Trade Commission, comprises a key component of online safety to consider when working with today's learners. Fundamentally, COPPA restricts the online collection of personal information from children younger than 13 years of age. While COPPA applies to US citizens and corporations, it effectively impacts people and corporations around the world.

COPPA overviews the responsibilities of online services and website operators as they structure privacy policies, the basics of obtaining verifiable consent from parents and guardians, and additional responsibilities of operators. Purposing to protect the online safety and privacy of children, COPPA also encompasses marketing limitations when involving children younger than age 13.

Figure 6.2. COPPA Overview. Video presentation explaining the Children's Online Privacy Protection Act

In the words of Wilson, Alaniz, and Sikora (2016),

> As guardians of the well-being of future generations, school stakeholders must consider strategies for involving students, parents, and community

members in developing a culture of online safety and digital citizenship, in K–12 settings and beyond. . . . Some schools and districts designate campus personnel, such as digital learning specialists or technology directors, as those responsible for reviewing the Terms of Service/Terms of Use and privacy policies of the websites teachers desire to use within their classrooms. (pp. 37–38)

Additionally, educators may be asked to play a more central role in this process, such as in the following examples:

> Faculty members may be invited to share suggested sites with these designated community members, allowing another set of eyes to review terms and privacy policies before new sites are introduced to the students. . . . These suggestions, of course, represent only a start to safeguarding students' online privacy and protection. Educational organizations, districts, and schools still need to deliver richer, more applicable teacher and parent education regarding the specifics of student data and privacy. (Alaniz, Wilson, & Sikora, 2016, pp. 38–39)

As time marches on, greater numbers of educators are capitalizing on the power of digital tools and resources to engage learners and to elevate learning experiences in ways that were not previously imaginable. Even while forward-thinking administrators, digital learning specialists, and professional development facilitators convey messages regarding digital innovation within school settings, educators on the front lines are still responsible for protecting learners' online safety.

The task of empowering students to be effective digital citizens becomes progressively more complex and challenging year after year. Expanding digital innovation across all fields—and specifically within educational settings—makes this priority even more imperative than ever before. Educators facing packed schedules and mounting pressures to bring about increased student achievement cannot take on the weight of this challenge single-handedly. This must be a collaborative endeavor involving educational administrators, directors of technology, digital learning specialists, and parents, all serving alongside educators to accomplish this crucial goal. In this case, as always, teamwork makes the dream work.

ESSENTIAL IDEAS TO REMEMBER

Before delving deeply into integrating digital tools and resources within assessment opportunities, educators must thoughtfully ponder certain important considerations. Educators play a vital role in guiding and empowering their students in safely and wisely leveraging digital tools and resources.

These considerations also include several crucial but often forgotten touchstones of our time, such as digital safety and coping with COPPA policies. As educators collaborate with educational leaders and parents to empower students in developing essential knowledge and skills surrounding digital citizenship, they more effectively prepare them to harness the vast potential of digital tools and resources to purposefully and beneficially impact society for years to come.

REFERENCES

Alaniz, K. (2021). *Collegial coaching: Mentoring for knowledge and skills that transfer to real-world applications.* Lanham, MD: Rowman & Littlefield Education.

Herring, M. C., Koehler, M. J., & Mishra, P. (2016). *Handbook of technological pedagogical content knowledge (TPACK) for educators* (2nd edition). New York: Routledge.

Juma, C. (2016). *Innovation and its enemies: Why people resist new technologies.* New York: Oxford University Press.

Koehler, M. J. (2012, September 24). *TPACK explained.* https://matt-koehler.com/tpack2/tpack-explained/

Koehler, M. J., & Mishra, P. (2009). What is technological pedagogical content knowledge? *Contemporary Issues in Technology and Teacher Education, 9*(1), 60–70.

Lei, J., & Zhao, Y. (2007). Technology uses and student achievement: A longitudinal study. *Computers in Education, 49,* 284–96. http://www.gram.edu/sacs/qep/ chapter%206/6_8Lei.pdf

Shulman, L. S. (1986). Those who understand: Knowledge growth in teaching. *Educational Researcher, 15*(2), 4–14.

Wilson, D., Alaniz, K., & Sikora, J. (2016). *Digital media in today's classrooms: The potential for meaningful teaching, learning, and assessment.* Lanham, MD: Rowman & Littlefield Education.

Chapter 7

Finding Joy in the Journey

How Can Authentic Assessment Impact Students' (and Educators') Enjoyment of Learning?

> *"Learning is not attained by chance.
> It must be sought for with ardor and attended to with diligence."*
>
> —Abigail Adams

When educators intentionally foster meaningful assessment practices within classroom settings, the entire learning environment is transformed. As students achieve developmental milestones, their enthusiasm often becomes contagious, thus inspiring them to apply their learning beyond the walls of the classroom. An investment in authentic assessment strategies holds the potential to profoundly and perpetually transform the culture of a classroom—and beyond that, a campus. Even more so, it indelibly impacts the lives of today's students.

Authentic assessment endeavors provide a vision and a pathway whereby educators can leverage applicable, meaningful learning adventures to profoundly benefit students' educational experiences. As learners engaged in authentic assessment experiences achieve student learning outcomes, their confidence and excitement for learning organically grow. They also become more likely to share their successes with others. The long-term impacts of authentic assessment experiences correlate with time-proven, research-based tenets of teaching and learning.

For instance, authentic assessment opportunities involve the Vygotskian principle known as the zone of proximal development. Across many years, innumerable educators have employed this concept through investigating learners' current developmental levels and their potential for further development in the future, thus allowing them to guide individual students in mastering increasingly advanced concepts and skills.

Thus, scaffolding profoundly impacts instructional endeavors. The zone of proximal development represents the space between a student's autonomous performance level and the subsequent level of supported performance, or what the learner can achieve with help. When utilizing authentic assessment methods, educators provide the scaffolding needed to bridge these gaps, linking the points between a student's abilities to demonstrate real-world knowledge and skills independently with the knowledge and skills yet to be mastered.

In addition to integrating the zone of proximal development, effective authentic assessment endeavors also feature reciprocal teaching opportunities, which align with Vygotsky's principles regarding the significant role of social engagement, or dialogue, in cognitive growth. In accordance with this theory, the processes of thinking aloud and talking through ideas encourage new insights to develop and allow for revisions of learning, thus enhancing cognition. Throughout reciprocal learning endeavors, intentional guidance and feedback must be offered to facilitate meaningful learning experiences.

In due course, learning expands as students engaged in reciprocal learning take turns serving as "the teacher." Authentic assessment endeavors provide learners with the opportunity to take turns being the instructor as well as the student, allowing all students to develop within these roles. Through experiences involving thinking aloud and discussing insights collaboratively, powerful reciprocal learning opportunities come about, benefitting all students along the way.

CULTIVATING THE JOY OF LEARNING THROUGH AUTHENTIC ASSESSMENT ENDEAVORS

For far too many students, learning is viewed as a "have to" instead of a "want to" in life. Countless learners (and their teachers) spend their school days awaiting the weekends, their weekends dreading the start of a new school week, their academic years awaiting the summer months, and their summer months dreading the start to a new academic year. They consistently count down the hours left in each school day and the days left in each school year. This reality seems especially heartbreaking when one considers how many waking hours the average student spends in school, assuming they spend eight hours per day sleeping (Wherry, 2004):

- 24 hours a day minus 8 sleeping hours = 16 waking hours a day
- 365 days a year × 18 years = 6,570 days
- 6,570 days × 16 waking hours = 105,120 waking hours by age 18
- The average child spends 6 hours a day at school for 180 school days a year
- 180 school days × 6 hours per day = 1,080 hours per school year
- 1,080 hours × 13 school years = 14,040 school hours
- 14,040 school hours divided by 105,120 waking hours

For some, 105,120 waking hours may not seem a significant amount of time in light of a lifetime of hours spent engaged in other pursuits. Yet, for a child, adolescent, or young adult who dreads attending school, 105,120 hours represent an astounding sum.

Nearly any adult can identify with the sense of discouragement that accompanies feeling "stuck" in a job involving seemingly meaningless work. Many adults can also relate to the feelings of inadequacy and frustration that result from a working environment where it seems impossible to succeed, let alone make progress toward advancement. Sadly, countless students feel exactly this way when their work at school seems purposeless or disconnected from their everyday lives outside of the classroom. Additionally, those who struggle with test-taking or battle testing anxiety may eventually begin to experience the frustration of feeling unable to succeed.

Authentic assessment addresses these far-too-common pitfalls within many educational settings by providing meaningful, applicable learning endeavors that offer more to work toward than "making the grade" on the next quiz or exam. In fact, authentic assessments directly relate to real life, empowering students to develop knowledge and skills that support their success in future academic, professional, and personal endeavors. Such assessment experiences promote engagement, enthusiasm, and enjoyment of learning, as they allow learners to capitalize on their interests and focus on their current or future pursuits, making every moment of discovery and creation more meaningful.

In the words of Professor John Wang (2017) of the National Institute of Education,

> When students look for "interesting" teachers and classrooms, they are in fact looking for an environment that caters to their core needs for autonomy, competence, and relatedness. They look for teachers who are able to meet their needs and interests and who can create interesting and challenging lessons that are relevant to their lives. A classroom where "joy of learning" exists is one in which students are given appropriate levels of challenges and one in which they are able to make decisions about their learning. . . . When they experience "joy of learning," students benefit from a positive learning experience. From the teacher's perspective, it would always be more rewarding if students were motivated and eager to learn: When teachers see motivated students, they too, become more interested to teach.

Authentic assessment endeavors not only make learning processes more joy-filled for students, they also bring greater joy and fulfillment for the educators facilitating those learning experiences. Rather than forcing educators to "teach to the test," authentic assessment endeavors encourage educators to facilitate applicable learning experiences that foster an environment of student innovation. As educators cultivate learning opportunities that transition students from consumers of information to architects of new learning experiences, they in turn encounter the joy of witnessing learners' creativity brought to life.

As students design unique artifacts of learning, the process of grading assignments encompasses greater joy for their teachers. Rather than using a Scantron or learning management system (LMS) to grade quiz after quiz or test after test in which every answer must be the same to be correct, grading authentic assessment endeavors is vastly different. With authentic assessment, every submission is unique. No two student products look the same, as each learner is responsible for designing an original artifact of learning. Grading becomes a joy as each new submission is distinctive; in many cases, educators witness elements unlike anything they have ever seen with the review of every new finished product.

A prevalent example of authentic assessment in action within EC–12 settings involves digital storytelling, which is the practice of utilizing digital tools and resources to tell stories. Such stories typically include a combination of text, narration, images, music, and videos to convey meaning. A variety of free, web-based tools exist for digital story creation, enabling learners of all ages to design meaningful artifacts of learning. As pre-service and in-service teachers within the authors' university are encouraged to incorporate digital storytelling into their assessment practices, their students benefit in profound ways.

For example, instead of asking students to write papers about the lives of famous children's authors, one second grade teacher led them in creating a collaborative digital story. Each student was responsible for researching and writing a script for one segment of a highlighted author's life before drawing a corresponding illustration. These images were then digitized and uploaded within a video creation tool, and each student was responsible for narrating their particular segment of the author's life story. The cohesive finished product, complete with text, narration, images, and music, represented a collaborative authentic assessment piece students (and their teacher) were delighted to view again and again! This is an assignment they will not easily forget, as together, they created a masterpiece they will cherish for years to come.

At the authors' university, the Master of Science in Learning, Technology, and Design program evidences these phenomena. This fully online program was designed to equip aspiring instructional designers and educational leaders with the knowledge and skills necessary to bring transformative leadership to today's dynamic academic and professional landscapes. The courses in the program do not require textbooks; learners obtain every resource needed, including articles, websites, and videos, from the learning management system in which the program is housed. This allows for consistently updated, applicable resources to be presented throughout the program.

The program contains no quizzes or tests; rather, every authentic assessment opportunity presented throughout the program is directly applicable to students' current or future professional endeavors. Learners create artifacts of learning that address student learning outcomes throughout each course, and every assessment opportunity is designed in an open-ended format, in order that students experience the joy of designing finished products that can be immediately applied to their professional contexts, even within the upcoming days or weeks.

For example, as students learn about new adaptive technologies in a course called "Current Topics in Learning with Technology," one assignment involves creating a video tutorial that overviews the features and applications of an adaptive learning tool students can utilize within their professional settings. Learners share their video tutorials within a discussion board forum before viewing and offering feedback regarding other tutorials created by colleagues. In this way, they collaboratively create a curated collection of applicable, original video tutorials. Students also engage in a reciprocal learning experience as they teach one another about innovative applications of adaptive technologies. They actively reflect upon their learning as they discuss new insights through their discussion board forum comments and questions.

The courses within the program were created to equip instructional professionals in a variety of settings with knowledge and skills directly applicable to their future lives, both in the workplace and beyond. Each course contains intentionally embedded, highly relevant authentic learning experiences to prepare for meaningful employment in educational institutions, corporations, nonprofit organizations, and government agencies. The process of engaging in innovative course design and facilitation has been a tremendously rewarding experience for the course designer, as well as for the students.

Each assessment piece includes a written description as well as a video explanation intended to guide students in grasping the WHY, or purpose, for engaging in that particular assignment. Exemplars for assessments also encourage and empower students to begin with the end in mind, working toward clear goals with intentionality and excellence.

Feedback from student evaluations suggests that the students genuinely appreciate the opportunity to engage in applicable learning experiences:

- "This course was wonderful. . . . I found the coursework both engaging and challenging, and I especially enjoyed that the materials created within this course could be used within my own teaching career. It never felt like completing work for the sake of completing work."

- "I enjoyed that this class had direct application within our work or teaching environment. I was able to use what I created in this class directly within my own teaching and reflect on it in practice, which I really enjoyed."
- "I felt that I learned many valuable skills and produced artifacts that I was proud to include in my digital portfolio. I always appreciate the ways in which [our professor] always makes her assignments directly applicable to the work we all do outside of the course."
- "Thank you for another great course! I was so grateful to learn about and practice collegial coaching and appreciate that we all had the freedom to implement these experiences in a way that worked best for each person's situation."
- "I definitely was worried about this class at first because I'm not great with technology, but [our professor] simplified each assignment and made it so easy to excel in the course! I also like how this course is project-based. I tend to forget information quickly after taking a test, so I love that this course allowed me to explore information in a way that allowed me to be creative, thus making me retain more."

As described by Wang (2017),

> When teachers are motivated to teach and students are motivated to learn, the classroom becomes a very pleasant environment. Students are subsequently more able to enjoy the learning process and become more engaged in the classroom. This creates a very positive learning environment where knowledge construction is enthusiastically facilitated by the teacher and joyfully engaged in by students. (p. 10)

ESSENTIAL IDEAS TO REMEMBER

Purposeful, applicable authentic assessment endeavors support educators in making the dream of joy-filled learning a reality for their students and for themselves. By beginning with the end in mind and starting with WHY (chapter 3), each new learning opportunity becomes infused with purpose. As educators seek to intentionally design assessment experiences that align with real-world pursuits, they more deliberately address skills needed by learners to succeed in life, both in the present as well as in the future (chapter 4).

When they utilize the following innovative formula for meaningful learning, educators more effectively position students to develop an intrinsic motivation for learning: authentic issues + authentic audiences + authentic assessment = authentic learning experiences (chapter 5). As tools of the digital age continue to profoundly impact educational environments, effective educators seek to incorporate technology in applicable ways, empowering creation, critical thinking, communication, collaboration, character, and citizenship. They do so while also preparing learners to effectively navigate the promises and pitfalls inherent in the use of such tools, supporting students in safely leveraging digital technologies for the better (chapter 6).

In the words of Socrates, "Education is the kindling of a flame, not the filling of a vessel." The power of authentic assessment lies in its ability to kindle a passion for purposeful, applicable learning endeavors, and ultimately, to fan the flame of lifelong learning. What greater gift could an educator—or their students—ever aspire to gain?

REFERENCES

Wang, C. K. J. (2017). The joy of learning: What is it and how to achieve it. *Exchange, 1*, 7–11.

Wherry, J. H. (2004). The influence of home on school success. *Principal, 84*(1), 6–7.

About the Authors

Katie Alaniz, Ed.D., serves as director of the Center for Learning Innovations and Teaching Excellence (C-LITE) at Houston Christian University, where she also teaches undergraduate and graduate education courses within the College of Education and Behavioral Sciences. As a teacher and digital learning specialist for over a decade in both public and private schools, including her service as a digital learning specialist at River Oaks Baptist School, Dr. Alaniz guides educators as they meaningfully integrate digital tools and resources within their classrooms. Dr. Alaniz has authored or coauthored a number of books, including *Naturalizing Digital Immigrants: The Power of Collegial Coaching for Technology Integration*; *Digital Media in Today's Classroom: The Potential for Meaningful Teaching, Learning, and Assessment*; *Collegial Coaching: Mentoring for Knowledge and Skills That Transfer to Real-World Applications*; and *The Maximizer Mindset: Work Less, Achieve More, Spread Joy*. Additionally, she has published academic articles on a range of topics and presented at a variety of educational conferences in the United States and abroad. Her primary research interests include authentic assessment, digital learning, collegial coaching, and teacher education. Dr. Alaniz and her husband Steven reside in Houston and together enjoy serving their community through a nonprofit outreach program called Apartment Life.

Kristie Cerling, Ed.D., serves as dean of the College of Education and Behavioral Sciences at Houston Christian University. Dr. Cerling has over 25 years of experience in public and private schools and higher education. She has consulted and presented on a range of topics in the United States and abroad including effective teaching strategies, leadership development, women in leadership, and Holocaust education. She believes that educators need community and that there is value in knowing how to build that community of support. Dr. Cerling continues to volunteer in area K–12 schools while teaching and leading. She lives with her husband and three children in Houston.

www.ingramcontent.com/pod-product-compliance
Lightning Source LLC
Chambersburg PA
CBHW030241170426
43202CB00007B/85